ELECTIONS

Published in association with the Centre for Canadian Studies at Mount Allison University. Information on the Canadian Democratic Audit project can be found at www.CanadianDemocraticAudit.ca.

Advisory Group

Titles

ELECTIONS

John C. Courtney

UBCPress

15 14 13 12 11 10 09 08 07 06 05 04   5 4 3 2 1

Printed in Canada on acid-free paper that is 100% post-consumer recycled, processed chlorine-free, and printed with vegetable-based, low-VOC inks.

National Library of Canada Cataloguing in Publication

Courtney, John C.
  Elections / John C. Courtney.

(The Canadian democratic audit ; 1)
Includes bibliographical references and index.
ISBN 0-7748-1101-3 (set). – ISBN 0-7748-0917-5 (bound); ISBN 0-7748-0918-3 (pbk) (v. 1)

1. Elections – Canada. 2. Representative government and representation – Canada.
I. Title. II. Series.

JL193.C679 2004   324.6'3'0971   C2003-907511-7

Canadä

UBC Press gratefully acknowledges the financial support for our publishing program of the Government of Canada through the Book Publishing Industry Development Program (BPIDP), and of the Canada Council for the Arts, and the British Columbia Arts Council.

The Centre for Canadian Studies thanks the Harold Crabtree Foundation for its support of the Canadian Democratic Audit project.

UBC Press
The University of British Columbia
2029 West Mall
Vancouver, BC V6T 1Z2
604-822-5959 / Fax: 604-822-6083
www.ubcpress.ca

To my friends and colleagues at the University of Saskatchewan, David Smith and Duff Spafford, and to the memory of the late Hans Lovink. The study of Canadian politics has been greatly enriched by their contributions.

Contents

Figures and Tables

Figures

Tables

FOREWORD

This volume is part of the Canadian Democratic Audit series. The objective of this series is to consider how well Canadian democracy is performing at the outset of the twenty-first century. In recent years, political and opinion leaders, government commissions, academics, citizen groups, and the popular press have all identified a "democratic deficit" and "democratic malaise" in Canada. These characterizations often are portrayed as the result of a substantial decline in Canadians' confidence in their democratic practices and institutions. Indeed, Canadians are voting in record low numbers, many are turning away from the traditional political institutions, and a large number are expressing declining confidence in both their elected politicians and the electoral process.

Nonetheless, Canadian democracy continues to be the envy of much of the rest of the world. Living in a relatively wealthy and peaceful society, Canadians hold regular elections in which millions cast ballots. These elections are largely fair, efficient, and orderly events. They routinely result in the selection of a government with no question about its legitimate right to govern. Developing democracies from around the globe continue to look to Canadian experts for guidance in establishing electoral practices and democratic institutions. Without a doubt, Canada is widely seen as a leading example of successful democratic practice.

Given these apparently competing views, the time is right for a comprehensive examination of the state of Canadian democracy. Our purposes are to conduct a systematic review of the operations of Canadian democracy, to listen to what others have to say about Canadian democracy, to assess its strengths and weaknesses, to consider where there are opportunities for advancement, and to evaluate popular reform proposals.

A democratic audit requires the setting of benchmarks for evaluation of the practices and institutions to be considered. This necessarily involves substantial consideration of the meaning of democracy.

"Democracy" is a contested term and we are not interested here in striking a definitive definition. Nor are we interested in a theoretical model applicable to all parts of the world. Rather we are interested in identifying democratic benchmarks relevant to Canada in the twenty-first century. In selecting these we were guided by the issues raised in the current literature on Canadian democratic practice and by the concerns commonly raised by opinion leaders and found in public opinion data. We have settled on three benchmarks: public participation, inclusiveness, and responsiveness. We believe that any contemporary definition of Canadian democracy must include institutions and decision-making practices that are defined by public participation, that this participation include all Canadians, and that government outcomes respond to the views of Canadians.

While settling on these guiding principles, we have not imposed a strict set of democratic criteria on all of the evaluations that together constitute the Audit. Rather, our approach allows the auditors wide latitude in their evaluations. While all auditors keep the benchmarks of participation, inclusiveness, and responsiveness central to their examinations, each adds additional criteria of particular importance to the subject he or she is considering. We believe this approach of identifying unifying themes, while allowing for divergent perspectives, enhances the project by capturing the robustness of the debate surrounding democratic norms and practices.

We decided at the outset to cover substantial ground and to do so in a relatively short period. These two considerations, coupled with a desire to respond to the most commonly raised criticisms of the contemporary practice of Canadian democracy, result in a series that focuses on public institutions, electoral practices, and new phenomena that are likely to affect democratic life significantly. The series includes volumes that examine key public decision-making bodies: legislatures, the courts, and cabinets and government. The structures of our democratic system are considered in volumes devoted to questions of federalism and the electoral system. The ways in which citizens participate in electoral politics and policy making are a crucial component of the project, and thus we include studies of interest groups and political parties. The desire and capacity of Canadians for meaningful participation in public life is also the subject of a volume. Finally, the challenges and opportunities raised by new communication technologies is also considered. The Audit does not include studies devoted to the status of particular groups of Canadians. Rather than separate out Aboriginals, women, new Canadians, and others, these groups are treated together with all Canadians throughout the Audit.

In all, this series includes nine volumes examining specific areas of Canadian democratic life. A tenth, synthetic volume provides an overall assessment and makes sense out of the different approaches and findings found in the rest of the series. Our examination is not exhaustive. Canadian democracy is a vibrant force, the status of which can never be fully captured at one time. Nonetheless the areas we consider involve many of the pressing issues currently facing democracy in Canada. We do not expect to have the final word on this subject. Rather, we hope to encourage others to pursue similar avenues of inquiry.

A project of this scope cannot be accomplished without the support of many individuals. At the top of the list of those deserving credit are the members of the Canadian Democratic Audit team. From the very beginning, the Audit has been a team effort. This outstanding group of academics has spent many hours together, defining the scope of the project, prodding each other on questions of Canadian democracy, and most importantly, supporting one another throughout the endeavour, all with good humour. To Darin Barney, André Blais, Kenneth Carty, John Courtney, David Docherty, Joanna Everitt, Elisabeth Gidengil, Ian Greene, Richard Nadeau, Neil Nevitte, Richard Sigurdson, Jennifer Smith, Frank Strain, Michael Tucker, Graham White, and Lisa Young I am forever grateful.

The Centre for Canadian Studies at Mount Allison University has been my intellectual home for several years. The Centre, along with the Harold Crabtree Foundation, has provided the necessary funding and other assistance necessary to see this project through to fruition. At Mount Allison University, Peter Ennals provided important support to this project when others were skeptical; Wayne MacKay and Michael Fox have continued this support since their respective arrivals on campus; and Joanne Goodrich and Peter Loewen have provided important technical and administrative help.

The University of British Columbia Press, particularly its senior acquisitions editor, Emily Andrew, has been a partner in this project from the very beginning. Emily has been involved in every important decision and has done much to improve the result. Camilla Jenkins has overseen the copyediting and production process and in doing so has made these books better. Scores of Canadian and international political scientists have participated in the project as commentators at our public conferences, as critics at our private meetings, as providers of quiet advice, and as referees of the volumes. The list is too long to name them all, but David Cameron, Sid Noel, Leslie Seidle, Jim Bickerton, Alexandra Dobrowolsky, Livianna Tossutti, Janice Gross Stein, and Frances Abele all deserve special recognition for their contributions. We are also grateful to the Canadian Study of Parliament Group, which partnered with us for our inaugural conference in Ottawa in November 2001.

Finally, this series is dedicated to all of the men and women who contribute to the practice of Canadian democracy. Whether as active participants in parties, groups, courts, or legislatures, or in the media and the universities, without them Canadian democracy would not survive.

William Cross
Director, The Canadian Democratic Audit
Sackville, New Brunswick

Acknowledgments

The invitation from William Cross to join a team of fellow political scientists in an audit of Canadian democracy was too good to turn down. I am grateful to Bill for having asked me to become a part of this project and for having guided all of us through several collective meetings and various iterations of our respective tasks. Like students with an essay deadline looming, we were reminded with great tact (and a quiet forcefulness that Bill has mastered) that we had commitments to meet. It was a superb group to work with. I am thankful for our regular meetings over a two-year period, the helpful assessments we offered one another, and the friendships that were formed. Political science in Canada is a strong and proud profession which, as the Democratic Audit project bears witness, has a great deal to offer students, policy makers, and the general public. Bill Cross and the Canadian Studies Centre at Mount Allison University deserve full credit for having undertaken this initiative, the first of its kind in Canada.

Bill Cross, as it turned out, was only one-half of the team issuing directives, suggestions, and advice. The other half was Emily Andrew who, as senior editor at UBC Press, kept us fully informed about her views on the content of our individual undertakings and about the Press's standards and requirements. All who contributed to this series found Emily an absolute gem to work with. We are thankful for her contribution. I wish also to acknowledge my debt to Camilla Jenkins, who saw the manuscript through its final stages with the Press, and to Geri Rowlatt, for her preparation of the index.

I am grateful to my colleague Duff Spafford and to two anonymous readers for UBC Press for the suggestions they offered on an earlier draft of this book. I wish to acknowledge as well the support for the research stage of this book provided by the Social Sciences and Humanities Research Council of Canada and, through a grant from the Crabtree Foundation, Mount Allison's Canadian Studies centre.

I am indebted, once again, to the University of Saskatchewan. Since 1965, when I first joined its faculty, the university has been my home.

Students there, as elsewhere, are largely unaware of how their questions and interventions in lectures or seminars help to get the wheels turning in a professor's head. But the subjects I have set out to explore in *Elections* are in most cases those I have explored with students, often in response to questions they have raised in class. This book is aimed, as least in my mind, at answering some fundamental questions for future students in Canada who, like many others before them, are keen to learn about their electoral system.

If students have played a role in focusing my attention on the subjects canvassed in this book, so too have several of them contributed to the book's completion. I am grateful to Jim Farney, Megan Furi, William MacKinnon, Jenny Morton, and Jordan Valestuk for their research assistance. They proved, once again, that students whose interest has been whetted by a subject can often gather far more information on their assigned topic than can ever be used in a relatively short book! I trust they benefited from the experience nonetheless.

My greatest debt is to Dan Macfarlane, my principal assistant throughout the preparation of this book. Dan's willingness to tackle, sometimes on very short notice, a variety of questions demonstrated that he has a natural gift for research in the social sciences. A friendship formed, as was ours, in the course of academic research stands as one of the many rewards of life in a university.

Finally, to Helen, my thanks for the support and encouragement she has given throughout this project as well as earlier ones. Like her, that remains very special.

INTRODUCTION

A book auditing Canada's electoral system could be one of two kinds. It could be devoted largely, or even entirely, to an examination of our method of voting – the **plurality vote**. As "electoral system" is a term often used synonymously with "method of voting" such a book would seem at first glance to make a good deal of sense. Alternatively, the book could be more wide-ranging in its purpose and topics. It could explore all the principal components of the electoral system: not only plurality voting but also the franchise, electoral districting, voter registration, and electoral management. I call these the five pillars or building blocks of democratic elections in Canada.

It strikes me that a more wide-ranging book is preferable to one focusing exclusively on the method of election, for two reasons. First, there is already a considerable literature on the plurality vote in Canada. With few exceptions it follows a standard pattern: an account of the strengths and weaknesses of plurality voting is followed by a call to reform the method of election. Not much would be gained by writing another book along these lines. Major works on the topic of Canadian electoral reform are listed in the Additional Reading section. Second, the question underlying the Canadian Democratic Audit series amounts to this: what is the state of democracy in Canada? So far as Canada's electoral system is concerned, I believe there is just one way to try to answer that question. An audit must examine the five essential parts of federal, provincial, and territorial elections in this country.

In the final analysis, I conclude that four of the five components (the franchise, electoral districting, voter registration, and election management) have changed immeasurably from the time of Confederation and that without exception these changes have vastly improved the way elections are conducted in Canada. Collectively they place Canada at the forefront of democratic nations. The building block that has remained unchanged since Confederation is, of course, our plurality vote system. Plurality voting has become once again the subject of controversy and is now the focus of Canada's electoral reform movement. The contrasting history of the four building blocks, on the one hand, and the method of voting, on the other, raises a question at the heart of the Democratic Audit exercise: why are some institutions and institutional arrangements amenable to change and others not?

In the answer to that question lies an important clue as to why our plurality vote system has operated unaltered for more than 135 years. By definition methods of election are different from, let us say, who gets to vote or how elections are managed, for they are intimately intertwined with governance, representation, and the party system. They are a part of how parties, candidates, leaders, and voters connect at election time. To account for the strengths and weaknesses of plurality voting and call for a change in the system is relatively easy in isolation from the representational, governmental, and, possibly, constitutional consequences of changing methods of election. In contrast, this book raises questions that generally do not constitute part of the conventional wisdom about electoral reform, questions based on the view that at the core of our method of election there lies a complex relationship among plurality voting, party politics, and parliamentary representation. Readers, in turn, are left at the end of the exercise to judge for themselves how best to answer the call to replace our plurality vote.

My own view, which I would be the first to acknowledge is not shared by all my colleagues in Canada's political science community, is that caution is in order. It is not hard, as we shall see in Chapter 6, to find fault with plurality voting. The far more difficult part of the exercise comes in addressing two pressing questions: what kinds of reform should be implemented, and what are the likely consequences of the change? So far as the first of these questions is concerned, there is no agreement to date on an electoral method that would be better than the current one. With respect to the second, in many ways more troubling, question, we are far from understanding the impact of a move away from plurality voting on our representational practices, party system, and governance. With careful forethought, political institutions such as voting systems can be changed. But the fallout from those changes cannot be foretold with any great accuracy, and the expected benefits to be derived from a change do not always materialize.

This book was in its final stages at the Press when the Progressive Conservative and Alliance parties merged in late 2003. The merger, in effect, acknowledges that plurality elections offer an inducement to opposition parties garnering comparable shares of voter support and occupying roughly similar ideological space to join forces rather than to continue to compete with one another. By contrast, there is less incentive for parties to merge in proportional electoral systems, in which, over a series of elections, parties are more likely to strive to preserve their distinctive identity and to try to maintain the loyalty of their respective electoral clientele.

ELECTIONS

THE RULES OF THE ELECTORAL GAME 1

If, in the early twenty-first century, Canadians could magically return to the 1860s and begin, once again, the job of creating our country's political institutions, we would surely construct a number of them differently. On the legislative side, an elected upper house would almost certainly be favoured over a senate whose members were appointed by the prime minister. The powers now exercised by the cabinet, and particularly by the prime minister in his or her own right, might well be less extensive than is now the case. So far as federalism is concerned, the constitutional distribution of powers might better match taxing authority with spending powers suitable to a complex modern state in which two levels of government share responsibility for a wide range of public policies.

On the electoral front, at least some elements of the method of conducting elections, whose origins in several cases can be traced back to pre-Confederation colonial regimes, might not remain as they are currently constituted. At the top of the list for some Canadians would be our **first-past-the-post** (FPTP) system, or plurality voting, in which a seat is won by the candidate garnering the most votes, though not necessarily a majority. This method of electing members of parliaments and legislatures suited the understanding of electoral politics and the nascent two-partyism of the 1860s. But plurality voting has come in for some heavy sledding recently. The three federal elections between

1993 and 2000 produced a Commons of five parties, each drawing a disproportionate measure of its support from a different region. Because the relationship between votes cast for a party and the number of seats won was often oddly skewed, critics of the first-past-the-post method of election have called for its replacement with a more proportionate electoral system.

Apart from plurality voting the Canadian electoral regime has changed in several significant ways since Confederation, almost always for the better. Our franchise regulations grant the vote to all but a few adult citizens; the power to conduct periodic redistributions of electoral districts has been given up by the politicians and turned over to independent commissions; and nonpartisan officials routinely administer elections. All of these practices were unimaginable in the formative stages of the Canadian political system. Now they are taken as fundamental elements of open and participatory elections.

The unchanged plurality vote system stands as an exception to the general trend toward reforming Canada's electoral regime over the past 135 years. The system's opponents see this as a failure of Canadian democracy. Their claims against first-past-the-post are based on a particular understanding of democracy. Their principal charge is that first-past-the-post elections produce legislatures and parliaments that are less representative, responsive, and inclusive than would be the case with a more proportional electoral scheme. Caution is urged in accepting all the criticisms at face value, however, for it will be argued that the critics fail to consider the implications of change for all aspects of Canadian democracy. These include the larger questions of governance, representation, and accommodative political parties. That being said, those who criticize plurality voting speak in terms that resonate with at least some members of the public.

Throughout this book, the changes made since Confederation to our electoral regime, along with the current criticisms of plurality voting, are discussed in relation to Canada's electoral system as a whole. The analysis employs the three principal criteria common to the entire Democratic Audit project: participation, responsiveness, and inclusiveness. This assessment of Canada's electoral system draws as well on the important related concept of representation, which in turn calls for a brief analysis of society's principal representative agents – political parties.

In any audit, fundamental costs and benefits are weighed in the balance. So far as Canada's electoral system is concerned this means measuring the appropriateness to Canadian society of its basic elements. In sum, the audit carried out here covers five different but nonetheless essential parts of Canada's electoral regime. They are, in order of the chapters that follow, the franchise, electoral districting, voter registration, electoral machinery, and the plurality vote. A final chapter draws the various parts of the analysis together with an exploration of the question of why some electoral institutions have been reformed and others not.

Elections: The Linchpin of Democracy

Elections are a key element of any political system that claims to be democratic. Without procedures and machinery that are known to be fair and equitable, the electoral process falls into disrepute and its results are treated with contempt. The rules of the electoral game therefore matter profoundly to a political system's legitimacy. Elections are, in a sense, the linchpins of the political process, linking government to the public pressures expressed by citizens, parties, interest groups, and social movements. Elections are also the basic mechanism holding a government accountable for its policies and actions. Our principal task will be to assess Canada's record on this front – to step back and take a look at where we were, how far we have come, and what, if anything, remains to be done with our electoral regime.

Elections in democracies can be distinguished from those in nondemocratic regimes by the rules, procedures, and regulations that govern their operation, and by the freedom with which the principal participants – citizens, candidates, and parties – can formulate and express their interests irrespective of the government of the day. A democracy, by definition, ensures that open and competitive elections for public office are held on a more or less regular basis without either state interference in the electoral process or police and military intimidation of parties, candidates, citizens, and means of communication. The same cannot be said of dictatorial or totalitarian systems. In those regimes no doubt exists about the outcome of carefully orchestrated, government-controlled exercises that, in the end, amount to little more than electoral travesties.

In a democracy, elections perform many essential tasks. They play a central and crucial role in the operation of government and in defining the institutional framework within which day-to-day governing takes place. As well, they ensure that different political and social views can be expressed freely, thereby contributing to a country's political stability and its degree of social cohesiveness. The flip side of that last point, however, is sometimes readily apparent. Free and democratic elections may work against stability and cohesiveness if some interests - regional, linguistic, religious, and so on - find that elections offer no satisfactory way of expressing their views, of advancing their cause, or of converting electoral support into legislative presence. If the rules of the electoral game are seen as favouring the interests of some groups over others, the electoral system may become an object of criticism. The validity of such criticisms must be judged in relation to the larger questions of governance, social tolerance, and regime stability.

Free and democratic elections do more than flesh out the institutional skeleton of government or enable individual and collective interests to be represented. They contribute in a major way to the number and configuration of political parties. Parties, having chosen leaders and candidates, are called upon to compete periodically in democratic elections under a set of election rules. Ostensibly, the purpose of most parties is to win office and form the government. Realistically, the best that the great majority of political parties can hope for is to gain sufficient support to influence the political agenda and public policy.

As a consequence the electoral system plays a critical part in determining how political preferences will be aggregated and represented. How many parties will there be in a country? Will they be ideologically driven? Will they be class-based? Will they be centrist and accommodative of otherwise conflicting social interests? What incentives does the electoral system offer for the creation of new parties or the amalgamation of old ones? These and other questions remind us of the close links that exist between the concept of representation and electoral and party systems in any democracy.

Finally, when elections operate as theory suggests they should, they contribute to a sense of citizen efficacy in the larger political system. Having cast a vote in a free and democratic election, a citizen should, as the election day draws to a close, believe he or she has made a contribution to the governance of society. This in many ways is the most elusive and intangible of purposes served by democratic elections, for it clearly involves several calculations, both personal and group, about the meaning that the results convey to citizens. How citizens see their electoral contribution to the larger process of governance will in large measure shape their individual perceptions of the responsiveness and inclusiveness of the system. If, for example, the gap is slight between the parties' respective share of votes in an election and their share of seats in a legislature, that can be expected to contribute to a greater measure of citizen support for the election outcome than if the gap had been substantial.

A citizen's respect for government and the outcome of an election is very often tied directly to the capacity of an electoral system to produce a stable majority government. In Canada there have been several instances of obvious discrepancies between a party's share of the votes and its share of the seats. Yet majority governments remain the norm here and levels of respect for "government," as opposed to a particular "party government," remain high. In contrast, elections in Israel, conducted under a strict proportional representation formula, produce virtually no gap between the various parties' share of votes and seats. Yet the citizenry's respect for election outcomes and government generally in Israel falls far below that in Canada. Indeed, Canadian surveys have found that popular support for recently elected governments generally goes up following an election. This suggests that independent of the level of popular support for a particular government, Canadians maintain respect for the electoral system in spite of its deficiencies.

Where the individual citizen fits into the electoral equation is critical in determining how "democratic" an electoral system is. For the concerns of citizens to be addressed as fully and as reasonably as possible by the institutions of government, the electoral system itself must first try to ensure a substantial measure of citizen inclusiveness, responsiveness, and participation in the process. Possibly more than any other institution of government, elections offer citizens the chance, however slight it may seem to many at the time, to influence government formation and, ultimately, policy outcomes. In that sense, elections are the pre-eminent means by which citizens and governments "connect." If the electoral system fails to meet that objective, then it contributes to a certain disconnect between citizens and their governments.

Bearing in mind the various roles outlined above that an electoral system is expected to play, this book's purpose is to reflect on the state of Canada's electoral regime. In keeping with the "audit" theme, the book offers an assessment of our electoral regime on a number of fronts. Obviously the most critical element of that assessment is to judge the adequacy and the appropriateness of Canada's current electoral institutions as the means whereby citizens can connect with their government. Simply put, are our laws and practices up to the job of ensuring that citizens accept elections as fairly representing their interests and of enabling them, should they chose, to participate fully in the electoral exercise?

Questions will also be explored about the capacity of the electoral system to contribute to a stable yet responsive set of representative institutions. The link between Canada's electoral and its party systems clearly should be examined. What are the consequences of having a method of election that discriminates, sometimes capriciously, among the country's political parties? In converting votes into seats, Canada's plurality vote system has generally favoured broadly based, nationally accommodative parties and regionally strong ones. What cost has this consequence of plurality voting had for other parties, which have sometimes been able to demonstrate having been disadvantaged by the way in which votes have been converted into seats? Is this differential treatment of party support a sufficiently serious problem to warrant changing our method of election? From the citizen's perspective, are there other critical issues of system responsiveness and inclusiveness that ought to be considered in assessing the plurality vote system? Are there countervailing issues of government stability and the type of party system best suited to Canadian society that should also be factored into the analysis? These and other questions inform the analysis of the five electoral building blocks in the following five chapters.

Voters

The franchise is clearly at the foundation of any electoral system. Citizens lacking the right to vote, no matter how informed they may be about public affairs or active in support of parties or candidates seeking public office, cannot participate in the most basic democratic exercise. By establishing who is entitled to vote and who is ineligible to vote in Canada we will learn a great deal about our electoral system, our changing social attitudes, and our courts as protectors of our electoral rights. In order to assess systematically this aspect of Canada's electoral system, Chapter 2, like the others, will develop its analysis historically. In terms of the franchise, this means accounting for the changes in the definition of who, among the various groups that collectively make up Canadian society, has been entitled to vote over time.

We will see that there has been a profound change in how Canada has defined the right to vote since our first post-Confederation elections.

The changes in the definition of who has been allowed to vote in this country may be greater than in any of the other building blocks of our electoral regime. Not only was the franchise limited to a much smaller proportion of citizens after Confederation, but in practical terms the early franchise at both the federal and provincial levels was not necessarily what the laws specified it to be. An elector's name may or may not have appeared on the lists depending upon such factors as the political circumstances in a riding, the party in control of the local machinery, and the known political allegiance of the voter.

This arbitrariness, which was the product of an exceedingly partisan approach to granting or denying the vote, stands in marked contrast to our current franchise laws. The contemporary franchise requirements at both the federal and provincial levels have resulted since the mid-1980s from a liberal interpretation by the courts of the Charter's protection of the right to vote. Before that, for the entire pre-Charter twentieth century, the reforms that were made to Canada's franchise laws reflected gradually changing social attitudes and values as well as a clearly diminished manipulation by governments of electoral laws for partisan purposes.

Electoral Districts

In a single-member district system, electoral districts enable voters to exercise their franchise and members to be elected. Accordingly, Chapter 3 examines electoral constituencies as an essential building block in the representational process. The importance of constituencies has never been far from the minds of politicians, and the party in power or, for that matter, all the parties in a Parliament or legislature, have sometimes abused their position to construct districts with political self-interests as the guiding principle. The periodic boundary readjustments throughout Canada's first century demonstrate how much more weight politicians were prepared to attach to their own political survival than to the larger public interest. Inequities in district population size were the obvious result of the time-honoured process of "gerry-mandering" constituency boundaries employed regularly by Canadian politicians, regardless of party stripe.

Not until the 1960s when, as has often been the case with both social and institutional reforms, Ottawa followed the lead of one province (in this case Manitoba) in adopting legislation that ensured decennial reviews of electoral districts, was the drawing of our territorially defined constituencies carried out by independent commissions. By the end of the twentieth century the practice of assigning boundary readjustments to nonpartisan agents had spread to all provinces and territories. The reforms meant a sacrifice on the part of the politicians, and proved that elected officials will on occasion subordinate their own interests to the public interest when a compelling case can be made for a fundamental structural change. The success of the move to independent electoral boundary commissions can be judged by the electoral fairness that has marked federal and many provincial redistributions since the 1960s. The independent boundary process is now open to citizen participation through local public meetings, a sign that the move away from politician-controlled redistributions to independent commissions has the potential to ensure as participatory a process as the public chooses to make it. The change has considerably improved our democratic electoral regime.

The issue of electoral equality was addressed in the early 1990s when the Supreme Court of Canada established what it asserted were the basic principles inherent in the Charter's right to vote provision: "effective representation" and "relative parity of voting power." The Court's decision stands unchallenged more than a decade later. It informs us about the representational and democratic standards the Court deemed appropriate to the construction of electoral constituencies in Canada. Because its terms are open to various interpretations, this decision left the door open to competing notions of what constitutes electoral fairness in Canada. That was sufficient to lead to a Charter challenge to Canada's plurality vote system early in the twenty-first century on grounds that among other things the effect of our method of voting has been to discriminate against women and minorities. Like the plurality vote, single-member districts, such as those traditionally designed in Canada, fashion political represen-tation along a territorially constructed dimension. The system's capacity to respond through territorially constructed districts to non-territorially based interests is worth exploring.

Voter Registration

Chapter 4 analyzes another of Canada's electoral building blocks, our method of registering voters. A generous franchise law may cast a wide net over a country's citizens, but without an adequate means of ensuring that those who are eligible to vote are in fact registered, the franchise itself is worth little. For most of the twentieth century, the lists of electors at both the federal and provincial levels in Canada were compiled shortly before an election through a state-operated, door-to-door enumeration. That has now given way to a more techno-logically driven approach to preparing and maintaining an electoral roll in the form of a so-called permanent registry of electors.

Any evaluation of the appropriateness to Canadian society of either system of voter registration must rest to a sizable degree on the issue of inclusiveness. Has one method an advantage in producing as com-plete a list of voters as possible? The case for one over the other rests as well on the more subtle and indirect contribution that an electoral registration process can make to a democracy. Is door-to-door enumer-ation better suited to informing voters of a pending election and of their civic duty to participate in it? Can citizen engagement and voter participation in elections be better promoted by one method of voter registration over another? These questions about the impact of struc-tural or institutional changes on citizen participation and engage-ment in politics are rarely raised or taken into account by policy makers, yet they deserve our attention.

Managing Elections

In Chapter 5 we see how far the management of Canadian elections has come since Confederation. When the Canadas, New Brunswick, and Nova Scotia formed a federal union in 1867, each of the colonies brought with it a particular set of rules and regulations to govern the conduct of elections. The result, at least for Canada's first few elections, amounted to a grab bag of new federal and old colonial/provincial laws. The degree of decentralized administration for the first few federal elections was extraordinary by today's standards. The current laws and administrative practices governing federal elections are now quite the reverse of what they were in the last third of the nineteenth century. Federal elections have become highly centralized operations and an exception to the common claim that with the passage of time Canada has become one of the most decentralized federations in the world.

Canada's early post-Confederation election administration was markedly different from how elections are conducted now, at both the federal and provincial levels. Voting in early federal elections took place over several weeks, with access to polls and hours of voting varying from one province or constituency to another. Today voting takes place across the country or in each of the provinces and three territories on the same day. All polling stations, now vastly greater in number and accessibility than ever before, open for the same length of time. For over fifty years after Confederation, candidates could run for Parliament in as many constituencies as they chose. This practice of hedging their electoral bets served the interests of a number of members, including the prime ministers John A. Macdonald, Wilfrid Laurier, and Robert Borden. Members who were successful in two or more seats were expected to resign all but one before entering Parliament, although there were instances of MPs (notably Laurier from 1911-17) holding two seats for an entire Parliament. Even though the member elected in two districts cast only one vote in the assembly, the practice, clearly undemocratic by today's standards, is no longer allowed.

Provincial and federal elections in the early post-Confederation period were much more convergent in structure and personnel than is now the case. The same officials were used for elections at both levels. The qualifications for electors in federal elections were determined by provincial laws, which effectively meant that someone entitled to vote in a federal election in one province might not meet the eligibility requirements in another. In Ontario and Quebec an elected member could serve simultaneously in the provincial legislature and the federal Parliament, as illustrated by the post-Confederation career of John Sandfield Macdonald. Elected in 1867 to Queen's Park (where he became Ontario's first premier) and to Parliament, Macdonald served in both federal and provincial assemblies until his death in 1872.

These practices remind us how partisan, varied, and politically self-serving Canada's electoral machinery was in the country's first few decades. It was a far cry from the electoral laws and administrative organizations we now have in place federally, provincially, and territorially. Like the franchise, the administration of our elections has been substantially improved at both levels of government. The integrity of Canada's electoral machinery is now an accepted (and expected) part of the country's political fabric. The fair and impartial management of elections, which has become one of the hallmarks of elections in Canada, has helped to ensure orderly transfers of power in this country. This has not escaped the attention of the larger international community. Election officials from Canada are frequently called upon to help organize elections or to serve as impartial, experienced election observers in emerging democracies. That speaks well of electoral administration in Canada.

Plurality Voting

Chapter 6 is devoted to an analysis of our first-past-the-post (FPTP) electoral system. The plurality vote system, as it is also known, translates the votes cast into parliamentary seats. In contrast to the franchise and other important components of our electoral regime, this aspect of our electoral system has barely changed since Confedera-

tion. Obviously the capacity of the political system and the willingness of the political elites to change key aspects of the electoral
regime are questions to be addressed, particularly as Canada's plurality vote system has, in the minds of some, cast a shadow over the legitimacy of elections in this country. Critics of plurality voting call for
fundamental changes to Canada's method of election. The current system's defenders, on the other hand, question whether the benefits of
any suggested reform would justify the risks to the larger political system. They believe electoral reform would hurt the ability of the major
parties to fashion broad intraparty coalitions of diverse regional and
social interests. They are also concerned about the possibility of
unstable coalition governments becoming the norm in Canada.

We will explore the arguments of those who call for the introduction of a different method of election and compare them with those in
favour of maintaining the current system. This will require an analysis of our concept of representation, the "democratic deficit" (of which
much is now heard), and the contexts of governance and representation within which any possible change to our electoral system should
be evaluated.

Aboriginals and the Canadian Electoral System

The inclusion and participation of Canada's Native people in elections
will be explored in various parts of the book. Aboriginal people have
been the neglected members of the larger electoral community. They
were the last Canadians to be granted the franchise and until recently
political parties made little attempt to recognize Aboriginal concerns
in their election platforms, to nominate Aboriginals, or to include Aboriginals in their party apparatus. Their participation rates, as measured by percentages of voter turnout figures, have been consistently
the lowest of any identifiable group in Canada. So too the nominations
of Aboriginals for election to federal or provincial assemblies have
been substantially below their share of Canada's total population.

Although there is a sizable Native representation in the legislature of the Northwest Territories, only in Nunavut (the one territory in which indigenous Canadians make up a clear majority of the total population) is the legislature composed of a majority of Aboriginals.

To add to the difficulties that Aboriginal people have faced in gaining the franchise and in getting nominated for public office, Canada's electoral system has worked against the interests of identifiable groups that are not geographically concentrated. Plurality voting with single-member districts has made it difficult in the past for widely dispersed, small population groups to gain the share of electoral representation they might have expected were their numbers highly concentrated in a relatively small area. Such has been the fate of Canada's Aboriginals, for they are spread thinly and unevenly across the country. However, most parties have begun deliberately attempting to broaden their demographic bases by nominating visible minority candidates for election to Parliament. Indeed, since the early 1990s various proposals have aimed at rectifying the underrepresentation of Aboriginal Canadians, who make up roughly 3.5 percent of Canada's total population, in Parliament. These have ranged from the creation of specially constructed Aboriginal electoral districts, to guaranteed representation in the Senate, to an elected Aboriginal parliament. None so far has been implemented. The strengths and weaknesses of the proposal relating to Aboriginal electoral districts will be discussed in Chapter 3.

Electronic Democracy and the Electoral Regime

Canadians are increasingly entering the "wired world." Advances in technology, coupled with attendant changes in the means of communication, have raised the prospect of technologically driven forms of democracy. The most obvious example to date is the changed method in the 1980s and 1990s for the selection of party leaders. Arguing that "one person, one vote" procedures were inherently more open and democratic than the delegated convention system, party organizers abandoned leadership conventions attended by hundreds, perhaps thousands, of voting delegates. They replaced this familiar institution with a so-called direct and unmediated voting that relied on newly available forms of electronic communication. A party's mass membership was thus entitled to vote directly for a new leader.

By way of Touch-Tone telephones, cellular telephones, and satellite-beamed television coverage, Canadian citizens could participate on their own, rather than through delegates, in the selection of party leaders. They could do this from the comfort of their own homes or at some distance from their regular residence. Although the record was mixed, generally the number of individuals participating directly in the exercise increased, in some cases substantially. Whether the enhanced levels of participation actually translated into an increased sense of citizen inclusiveness in the political process and of government responsiveness to citizen engagement remains an as yet unanswered question.

On a larger, but so far in Canada untried scale, electronic democracy could possibly be phased in for provincial and federal elections. Replacing, or more likely supplementing, such traditional and familiar symbols of voting as community polling stations, paper ballots, and pencils with something as dramatically different as Internet or Touch-Tone telephone voting from their home, office, or other location might introduce Canadian citizens to new ways of understanding democratic participation and involvement. What would the benefits and risks of such a change be? Would the availability of Internet voting in fact lead more Canadians to vote?

Canada's chief electoral officer has held out such a hope. He has asserted that being able to vote via the Internet would be particularly attractive to young Canadians – that is, to those who are now least likely to vote. But as with the changes introduced by parties for the selection of their leaders, the effect of electronic elections is as yet unknown. That is all the more reason why important issues of inclusiveness, responsiveness, and participation will have to be considered before massive, technologically driven changes in the electoral process are put in place. These changes will be more fully explored in Chapter 5.

Auditing Canada's Electoral System

It is important to ask how much reform there has been to Canada's electoral system, for what reasons the reforms were adopted, and what remains to be changed. How much has Canada's electoral system changed over time? The answer, in typically Canadian fashion, is "somewhat," with the needle pointing slightly in the direction of more rather than of less change. On the credit side of a democratic audit of Canada's electoral system stand several substantial reforms that have made the electoral system fairer, more transparent, and more open. These changes have affected parties and candidates, of course, but their major impact has been on the electorate. Voters now have demonstrably more opportunities to participate freely and fairly in elections in Canada than ever before. Laws, regulations, and, since the adoption of the Charter, courts have enhanced immeasurably the electoral system as an interrelated set of democratic structures and institutions.

The credit side of the audit would include Canada's electoral machinery and electoral offices, the franchise, and independent electoral boundary readjustments. These three elements of the larger electoral system are each markedly improved from what they were at the time of Confederation. None is perfect, nor is perfection likely given the trade-offs and ambiguities that are part of any democratic system. Still, to judge the extent to which electoral practices and laws have changed, we need only remind ourselves of the unsavoury sides of these elements 135 years ago. Canada's early elections were marked by arbitrary enfranchisement practices, partisan election officials, uncontrolled expenditures, including widespread bribery, and gerrymandered electoral districts.

That is no longer the case, and where problems may still occur, as for example with improper candidate and party fundraising and expenditures, laws are in place to seek prosecution of the offenders. In sum, a report card issued in assessment of these three elements could reasonably be expected to include grades in the top A range for the franchise, mid-A for election machinery, and B+ to A– for the independent electoral boundary readjustments. Although these are better than average grades, some still show room for improvement.

It is too early to evaluate the replacement of election-driven, door-to-door enumerations for registering voters with a continuous electoral roll, and the shift toward unmediated democracy. Whether the so-called permanent list will ensure greater voter inclusiveness, and whether it will reduce citizen engagement in the political process, can be known only with time. We may find that the switch from in-person enumerations toward technologically driven direct democracy does little to address the declining voter interest in politics and elections in the long run.

Regarding Aboriginal participation and inclusiveness in the electoral system, in the past the assigned grade has languished in the failing range, for there is little question that Canada's indigenous peoples have been the worst served of any group by our electoral system. The record of Aboriginal participation (as voters, candidates, and elected members) speaks volumes about the failure of successive governments and parties to design policies and programs aimed at ensuring Aboriginal inclusion in the political system. Only in the late twentieth century was the issue broached in any serious fashion; so far it has been without a satisfactory conclusion.

Plurality voting, possibly more than any other part of Canada's electoral regime, has provoked intermittent but usually heated controversy since the late nineteenth century. Reflecting our changing social values and attitudes, the grounds for criticizing plurality voting have broadened in the post-Charter era. The critics of plurality voting are now louder than they have been for many decades. Electoral reformers fault the current method of voting for contributing to representational imbalances, in strict numerical terms, in parliamentary caucuses and cabinets and to what they see as heightened sectional tensions in Parliament and around the cabinet table. Some also attribute to plurality voting the election of a smaller share of women and minorities to Parliament than their share of the total population would suggest. Yet in spite of the heavy academic, media, and political artillery that has been lined up against plurality elections in Canada, nothing has changed since 1867.

This raises an obvious question. Why has reform of some of the building blocks of our electoral system been possible (voter registration, election administration, and district boundary readjustments come immediately to mind), whereas reform of the method of election has so far eluded us? The concluding chapter tackles that question with the intention of describing the variables or conditions that would have to be met before changes to democratic institutions such as our method of election can be achieved. Chapter 7 also examines the pros and cons of compulsory voting in Canada and will conclude with a comment on plurality voting and Canadian democracy.

It would be a mistake to speculate too freely about the presumed benefits of a different method of voting within which the Canadian electoral system operates. Institutional changes often have unintended consequences. Furthermore, democratic representation, parliamentary institutions and practices, and the party system all have a history of well over a hundred years in Canada. They have become part of our electoral fabric, a fact that should not be taken lightly. To think that all of these will be improved by a different method of election places an immense, and possibly unwarranted, stress on the presumed benefits of institutional transformation. How a different set of electoral rules might affect our system's capacity to sustain an impressive measure of responsiveness, inclusiveness, and citizen participation, as well as its continued ability to ensure a representational process that accommodates, rather than exacerbates, social differences and regional tensions, forms an essential part of our electoral scorecard.

Chapter 1

- Canada's electoral system includes five building blocks: the franchise, electoral districting, voter registration, electoral administration, and the method of voting.
- This audit of Canada's electoral system is based on three criteria: participation, inclusiveness, and responsiveness.
- Elections are the pre-eminent means by which citizens and governments connect with one another.

2 WHO CAN VOTE?

Throughout Canada's history, the evolution of our franchise has reflected the view expressed by Lord Sankey of the Judicial Committee of the Privy Council that the Canadian constitution was a "living tree capable of growth and expansion within its natural limits" (*Edwards v. A.G. for Canada* 1930). At the time of Confederation, for many Canadians voting was a privilege, not a right. The perception of voting was that it should be the right of those individuals who had both a stake in society and who were independent enough from the influence of others to participate in choosing the government. Accordingly, the vote was confined to male property owners twenty-one years of age or older. For many other groups, such as women, racial minorities, and Aboriginals, participation in the political process was merely an unattainable dream.

The picture did not remain this bleak. Between 1867 and 2002, voting in Canada evolved from being an elite practice open only to propertied males to a model of inclusiveness open to nearly all Canadians over the age of eighteen. This dramatic change was not the result of a master plan; instead, the franchise expanded in response to events and changing political values. The expansion of the franchise mirrored the growth of democracy and equality in Canada.

Yet the past growth and extension of the franchise must be considered in the context of a current paradox. The electorate is now larger and more inclusive of Canadian citizens than at any point in our history. But in federal and provincial elections of the past decade, there has been a significant drop in the share of the Canadian electorate that makes the effort and takes the time to vote. That voting is now more convenient and the ballot more accessible than ever before, because of advance polls, proxy voting, and some measure of overseas balloting, has compounded this puzzling picture. This chapter traces the evolution of the Canadian franchise from its primitive origins to the present. The analysis places the extension of the vote in the context of changing social and constitutional values, and offers some observations on the inclusiveness/participation paradox of contemporary Canadian democracy.

The Ballot in 1867

At the time of Confederation, Canadians followed the more traditional model of the British franchise, although they were also influenced by some democratic views that filtered into Canada from the United States. Lord John Russell spoke for many nineteenth-century British subjects on both sides of the Atlantic when he declared that universal suffrage "is the grave of all temperate liberty, and the parent of tyranny and license" (Garner 1969, 5). Universal manhood suffrage was associated with democracy, which in turn was seen in Britain as bringing disorder, demagoguery, and the excesses that had occurred in the American and French Revolutions. To prevent such evils, the right to vote was linked to property, status, and office.

The idea that voting rested in such externalities, and had nothing to do with the rights of citizens, was ridiculed by the eighteenth-century American politician Benjamin Franklin: "Today a man owns a jackass worth fifty dollars, and he is entitled to vote, but before the next election the jackass dies ... and the man cannot vote. Now gentlemen, pray inform me, in whom is the right of suffrage, in the man, or in the jackass?" (Garner 1969, 6). Franklin was referring to the

Enlightenment ideal that the right to vote was rooted in the freedom inherent in man's nature. That is, man was born free and freedom was a natural right of man. One way to protect that freedom was for man to have the right to choose those who governed him.

The Russell and Franklin views of the franchise were among those competing in nineteenth- and early twentieth-century Canada. Although the traditional view linking the franchise to property prevailed initially, as the nineteenth century wore on the idea that voting was a right that accrued to the individual became more widely accepted.

In 1867 the balance was clearly tipped in the direction of a restrictive view of the franchise. Section 41 of the British North America Act stated that provincial franchises would apply to elections of members to serve in the House of Commons until Parliament decided otherwise. For the Province of Canada (Ontario and Quebec as of 1867), this meant that every male British subject, aged twenty-one or more, being a householder, was granted the vote. Because the federal franchise was a matter of provincial jurisdiction, and because voters' qualifications varied from one province to another, until 1885 voter eligibility for federal elections differed across the country.

One constant throughout the country was that the right to vote was linked to property ownership, income, or other tangible signs of being independent and having a stake in the community. Among other things, property qualifications for voting meant that a man could vote in all the constituencies where he owned property. Moreover, until 1874 there was no secret ballot for voting, which meant that political organizers and others interested in how certain individuals voted could confidently and easily find out.

The restrictive nature of the franchise is demonstrated by the fact that between 1867 and 1891, an average of only about 20 percent of the total population was entitled to vote (Figure 2.1). The extent to which the Canadian electoral system was exclusive rather than inclusive was reflected in Manitoba, whose law establishing entitlement to vote was typical of other provinces. The requirement that a voter had to be of independent means was explained in the rules drawn up for Manitoba's

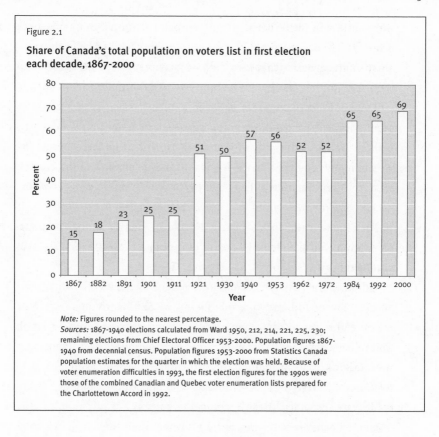

Figure 2.1

Share of Canada's total population on voters list in first election each decade, 1867-2000

Note: Figures rounded to the nearest percentage.
Sources: 1867-1940 elections calculated from Ward 1950, 212, 214, 221, 225, 230; remaining elections from Chief Electoral Officer 1953-2000. Population figures 1867-1940 from decennial census. Population figures 1953-2000 from Statistics Canada population estimates for the quarter in which the election was held. Because of voter enumeration difficulties in 1993, the first election figures for the 1990s were those of the combined Canadian and Quebec voter enumeration lists prepared for the Charlottetown Accord in 1992.

first election in 1870. The right to vote was granted to a householder, defined as follows: "Master or chief of a household; one who keeps house with his family. A householder does not mean a lodger, nor a tenant of part of a house, unless he has a separate maintenance and table enjoyed by himself and his dependants, distinct from other householders" (Donnelly 1963, 72 n. 2). A year later a statute described specifically the property qualifications required for voting in the province. Voters had to own property worth one hundred dollars, or had to be a tenant whose annual rent was at least twenty dollars. Property qualifications of this kind continued in Manitoba until 1888.

In all provinces there were four main criteria for voting. Electors had to be British subjects by birth or naturalization, male, property owners, and at least twenty-one years of age. Just as these standards of

Who Can Vote?

who could vote were defined by provincial statutes, the same laws often specified who could not vote. Many were excluded from the franchise on the grounds that they did not satisfy one or more of the main requirements for voting or did not possess the independent means and stake in the community believed to be necessary to vote. Government employees, government contractors, and judges and court officials, as well as those who worked as election officials, were denied the vote in many provinces on the basis that they depended on the government for their livelihood. The poor, or those who received social assistance, were not allowed to vote since they did not meet the criteria of either independence or of having a stake in the community. Not surprisingly given the strictly controlled franchise, criminals were also denied the vote.

Others were denied the vote on the basis of their race or national origins. Status Indians were unable to vote on the grounds that their treaty rights made them dependants of the government. In British Columbia, approximately one-half of the province's adult population in the 1870s was thus denied the franchise. In provinces like Ontario only "enfranchised Indians" – those who renounced their Indian status – could vote, provided that they met the property requirements. This presented Natives with the cruel choice between their Indian status and their right to vote. Few chose the latter (Minister of Public Works 1997, 46-7).

British Columbia also denied the vote to Orientals (a group defined initially as Chinese but later widened to include Japanese and other East Asians), a decision supported by John A. Macdonald. The prime minister asserted that persons of Chinese origin should not be allowed to vote because they had "no British instincts or British feelings or aspirations" (Roy 1981, 152). In the early twentieth century Manitoba introduced a "literacy test" that denied the vote to residents who had recently immigrated to Canada from the Ukraine and other central European countries even though many had become naturalized British subjects through immigration. According to the premier, such immigrants "take no interest in the affairs of this country and are incapable of learning about them" (Donnelly 1963, 73). The requirement that voters be British subjects with financial independence and a stake in the community was used to exclude many adults in Canada from the franchise.

Women were the largest group excluded from voting. In 1867 it was widely accepted that being male was an essential criterion for voting. The former colonies joining together in Confederation had, as a general rule, barred women from holding the franchise. Reflecting the attitudes of the time, the practice was based on the notion that women were not independent in their own right, but rather mere appendages of their fathers and husbands. It was also argued that voting was a rough and nasty business, particularly since violence often erupted at polling stations. Women, who were assumed to be delicate, were seen as unsuited to this kind of activity.

Religion was sometimes used to stress the subordination of women to men. For example, John Dryden, Ontario minister of agriculture in 1893, cited the Bible when he claimed that "man was not made for the woman but the woman for the man ... Thy desire shall be to thy husband and he shall rule over thee." Other arguments used against enfranchising women included the claim that voting would "unsex and degrade women, destroy domestic harmony, and lead to a decline in the birth rate" (Cleverdon 1974, 6).

The exclusion of women, East Asians, and Aboriginals were key features of the federal Electoral Franchise Act of 1885, the first statute establishing a uniform franchise across Canada. The Act was clearly a partisan document. The Macdonald government ensured that certain groups likely to support the Conservatives were given the vote for the first time. For example, many federal government employees and election officials, the majority of whom had received their office from the Conservatives, were allowed to vote in federal elections. However, judges, the vast majority of whom had been named to the bench by provincial Liberal governments, continued to be denied the vote. The legislation's property qualifications for voting were more favourable, on balance, to rural residents than to urban dwellers, a clear indication of where the Macdonald Conservatives saw their greatest electoral support lying.

A significant change was made in the compilation of federal electoral lists, which had previously been entirely in the hands of municipal employees. After 1885 the government (which, for all intents and purposes, amounted to the governing party) assumed the power to appoint the returning officers and enumerators responsible for deciding who would be on the voters list. This new system of compiling the electoral rolls opened the door to partisan abuses. In the 1891 federal election in Ontario, for example, 34,000 individuals who were dead or who had left the province were on the voters lists, whereas some 50,000 new voters could not exercise their franchise because their names were not on the lists (Minister of Public Works 1997, 44 and 48-52).

Following the 1896 election, the newly elected Laurier government set out to reform Canada's franchise. Under the Liberal legislation of 1898, control of the franchise and the electoral lists was returned to the provinces - a clear signal of where the Liberals' bias in electoral administration lay. The Laurier Liberals, strong proponents of provincial autonomy, supported the idea that provinces should control the federal franchise under guidelines established in the federal legislation. Equally important was that the Liberals handed over the federal franchise mainly to Liberal provincial governments. In at least two instances (Quebec and Nova Scotia) they shared Laurier's belief that the franchise belonged to those who owned property.

Some groups did not benefit from the 1898 changes and others were actually left worse off. Although the legislation stated that the provinces could not discriminate against "any class of persons," status Indians living on reserves were not considered to be covered by this guarantee and continued to be denied the vote. Manitoba, Ontario, and New Brunswick had in the past denied the vote to prison inmates, mentally handicapped people living in asylums, and those who received charitable assistance from the government. Those categories were added to the expanded list of excluded persons under the 1898 federal law. Thus in some ways the new provisions establishing the right to vote were more restrictive than previously.

Nonetheless, the overall effect of the 1898 changes was to make the Canadian electoral system more inclusive. At the provincial level, the traditional view that property and voting were inextricably linked had been replaced in most cases (Quebec and Nova Scotia being the exceptions) by the more democratic view that all male British subjects over twenty-one should have the vote. Because of the generously more liberal provincial franchise guidelines, the 1898 law granted the vote to some who had previously been denied it. Although they varied from one province to another, as a rule the newly enfranchised groups included certain provincial government employees and citizens of Chinese or Japanese ancestry. However, British Columbians of East Asian descent continued to be barred from voting in provincial elections for another half-century.

Women Gain the Vote

The biggest single factor promoting the inclusiveness of the electoral system was the enfranchisement of women. Although women did not officially receive the right to vote federally in Canada until 1920, some women did vote in the first half of the nineteenth century in parts of British North America. Colonial electoral practices were based on British models, which meant that only a common law tradition excluded women from the franchise. Colonial legislation, such as the 1791 Constitution Act creating Upper and Lower Canada, was silent on the issue of women voting.

Although the numbers were never large, there are documented cases of property-owning women exercising the franchise in pre-Confederation Canada. In Nova Scotia accounts of the 1840 election documented the competition for female votes. A contemporary observer stated that the Tories were working aggressively to win the election by "getting all the old women and old maids, and everything in the shape of petticoats, to be carried up to the hustings" (*Novascotian* 1840, quoted in Garner 1969, 156). Voting by women was most common in early nineteenth-century Lower Canada – present-day Quebec – partly because English common law traditions did not apply to the colony. In 1809 the mother of radical French Canadian politician Joseph Papineau voted for her son. Other women who began to vote in the 1820s followed her example and votes. The 1834 election in Lower Canada was actually contested on the grounds that it was invalid because women voted. A deliberate process was then begun of passing laws to exclude women from voting, with the result that the implementation of section 41 of the BNA Act in 1867 effectively denied the federal vote to women in Canada.

By the late nineteenth century, there was increasing pressure to extend the franchise to include women. American and British suffrage movements that linked voting to individual human rights influenced some Canadian women. They argued that all citizens, whether male or female, should have the right to vote as a "symbol of citizenship" (Prentice et al. 1988, 169). In 1871, for example, an American suffrage leader told audiences of Canadian women that they were "meek, milk and water and had no rights of their own" (Prentice et al. 1988, 175). In 1876 the Toronto Women's Literary Club was formed to discuss ways to advance the cause of women. The club increasingly devoted its efforts to pressing for the vote. Six years later the organization ended the pretence of being a literary society and transformed itself into the Canadian Women's Suffrage Association. By the turn of the century, a number of other groups had been established to promote the enfranchisement of women.

Although groups advocating women's right to vote were instrumental in bringing the issue of female suffrage to the public's and the politicians' attention, other pressure groups championing the vote for women soon surfaced. Widespread support for extending the franchise to women came more often from the development and evolution of various social reform organizations. As women became more involved in charitable organizations and movements to remedy the ills of society, they gained political experience. As early as the 1850s, women in Upper Canada had petitioned the government for changes in legislation. An early twentieth-century suffragist related the plight of "the racked and poverty burdened woman dwelling in a city tenement, with her brood of ill-nurtured, sickly children" to high taxes, low wages, and "liquor too near her husband's temptation." Alcohol was seen as the root cause of many social problems, and the campaign to end its use through prohibition meant that women had to become involved in politics.

The relationship between prohibition and the enfranchisement of women was shown in Manitoba, the first Canadian jurisdiction to give women the vote. In 1893 the Women's Christian Temperance Union (WCTU), which had been organized in Ontario in 1874 to press for prohibition, presented a petition to the Manitoba legislature supporting universal suffrage. Although the petition did not succeed, prohibition and female suffrage were thereafter linked. After the Liberals, who had supported both prohibition and female enfranchisement, were elected in Manitoba in 1916, a committee was established to prepare a question for a referendum on prohibition. The committee recommended that women be given the vote prior to the referendum on prohibition, an important factor in guaranteeing the referendum's success (Morton 1957, 348-9).

Other provinces quickly followed Manitoba's lead. Saskatchewan and Alberta granted the vote to women the same year, while women in Ontario and British Columbia were enfranchised in 1917. Nova Scotia granted the female franchise in 1918, New Brunswick in 1919, Prince Edward Island in 1922, and Newfoundland in 1925. In 1940 Quebec became the last province to grant women the vote, a reflection of the power of the Catholic church and the conservative social views that long dominated that province.

There were other reasons besides the temperance issue that women on the Prairies attained the right to vote before they did in other regions of the country. Settling the Prairies was a cooperative venture in which women played a major role. It should not be surprising, then, that farmers' organizations and reform parties such as the Progressives supported electoral reform. The 1916 Farmer's Platform, which was endorsed by farmers' organizations in Manitoba, Saskatchewan, and Ontario, supported extending the federal vote to women and allowing them to run in federal elections. Concerns about the electoral influence of the wave of immigrants from Eastern Europe also prompted support for female enfranchisement. As one Prairie reformer put it: "What an outrage to deny to the highest-minded, most cultured native born lady of Canada, what is cheerfully granted to the lowest-browed, most imbruted foreign hobo that chooses to visit our shores" (*Grain Growers Guide* 1909, quoted in Cleverdon 1974, 6). A final factor in the broad public support for giving women the vote in Manitoba was the sizable community of Icelandic settlers, whose traditions had long supported equal rights for women.

At the federal level, the Wartime Elections Act and the Military Voter's Act of 1917 enfranchised female relatives of men serving in the Canadian armed forces. They granted the vote as well to all serving in the military, including those not yet twenty-one years of age and Aboriginals. Practical politics as opposed to idealism underlay Canada's most controversial franchise legislation. The issue in the 1917 federal election was adoption of conscription as part of Canada's continuing war effort in Europe, a policy favoured by the Unionist government but opposed by the opposition Liberals. The legislation blatantly enfranchised groups who, in large numbers, would support the introduction of conscription. That included women. Many who were expected to vote for the opposition Liberals were denied the vote. This included conscientious objectors, British subjects naturalized after 1902 born in an enemy country or who habitually spoke an enemy language, and pacifist groups, such as Mennonites, Hutterites, and Doukhobors.

Despite the government's partisan intentions in enfranchising some women in 1917 as a temporary and politically expedient move, there was no turning back. The Borden government passed the Women's Franchise Act in 1918, thereby granting the vote to all women over twenty-one who met existing property qualifications according to their province's election law.

By the time of the next election in 1921 property restrictions had been removed, a standard federal franchise law had been passed (the Dominion Elections Act 1920), and, with the addition of female voters, the total electorate effectively doubled in size (Figure 2.1). Ironically, although the British and American suffrage movements had begun earlier than their Canadian counterparts and were more radical than those in Canada, Canadian women got the vote at the federal level sooner than their counterparts in either the United Kingdom or the United States. By 1921 Canada's franchise laws were on the road to becoming a model of inclusiveness, although there were still a number of hurdles to be overcome before something approximating a universal franchise was achieved.

Extending the Franchise

The Dominion Elections Act in 1920 repeated some of the electoral prejudices of Canada's earlier franchise laws while slightly enlarging the total number of eligible voters. On the one hand, the legislation upheld the exclusion of certain groups from voting. Citizens disenfranchised at the provincial level because of race or religion were still to be excluded federally, as were judges, prisoners, and the mentally incapacitated. On the other hand, the Dominion-wide franchise included for the first time those living in charitable institutions and Aboriginal veterans of the First World War. Perhaps most notably the 1920 legislation created the Office of the Chief Electoral Officer. This meant that an officer of Parliament whose selection and operation was free of partisan interference would henceforth carry out election administration at arm's length from the politicians.

The Depression and the Second World War did little to enhance Canadian attitudes toward targeted minorities. In some cases the exclusion of voters on the basis of race and religion actually increased. In 1944 Parliament amended the Dominion Elections Act to ensure that people of Japanese ancestry who were relocated from British Columbia to other parts of Canada were denied the vote in the provinces to which they were transported. For its part, British Columbia continued to discriminate in provincial elections against Chinese, Hindus (interpreted broadly to encompass many South Asian groups), and Japanese Canadians, including First World War veterans of Japanese ancestry.

Gradually over the twenty years following the end of the Second World War, all of the federal and provincial racial and religious discriminatory provisions were removed. In 1948 Japanese Canadians were once again given the federal franchise, and the last provinces discriminating against Asian Canadian voters soon followed suit. In the 1950s, provinces such as Manitoba and New Brunswick began extending the franchise to all Aboriginal peoples, including status Indians living on reserves. The enfranchisement of Aboriginals was completed at the provincial level in 1969 when Quebec granted the vote to its Aboriginal population. At the federal level, the Inuit, who had lost the federal franchise in 1934, were once again given the vote in 1950. And, finally, in 1960, under the direction of Prime Minister John Diefenbaker, who had long argued for granting the vote to Canadian status Indians, Parliament amended the Canada Elections Act to ensure voting rights for all Indians, the last of Canada's Aboriginals to be granted the right to vote.

The enfranchisement in the 1950s and 1960s at both the federal and provincial levels of several groups previously denied the vote confirmed that the social values of Canadians had started to change. Voters and policy makers were becoming more accepting of racial minorities. The wave of post-Second World War immigrants and refugees from Europe, the Caribbean, and Asia, combined with the early initiatives aimed at making Canada a more racially tolerant and consciously multicultural country, helped to create a context within which liberalization of the franchise laws could take place.

Making the Vote Accessible

As the franchise was being extended in postwar Canada, other reforms were making it easier and more convenient for Canadians to vote. Voting at advance polls, which had been available to specific groups such as commercial travellers, was extended to all Canadians in 1960. Proxy voting, which had been available only to military personnel since the Second World War, was extended in 1970 and 1977 to include voters in special circumstances such as northern camp operators, fishermen, and prospectors. In 1993 mail-in ballots were introduced to guarantee the vote to Canadians who, because of unusual situations, were unable to vote in person on election day. As well, all voting material was made available in both official languages, and, where numbers warranted, in First Nations languages. Those with disabilities could more easily exercise their franchise rights as provisions ensured that polling stations were wheelchair accessible.

In 1970, when Parliament lowered the voting age from twenty-one to eighteen, two million Canadians were added to the voters list in the largest increase in the franchise since the vote was granted to women a half-century earlier (Figure 2.1). The Trudeau government made its case for lowering the voting age on the grounds of heading off possible intergenerational strife. In the 1969 Speech from the Throne the government noted that "a disturbing element in many countries of the world has been the rising tide of unrest, particularly among young people." It reasoned that this heightened level of interest in public issues needed to be channelled into peaceful and constructive forms. This argument paved the way for lowering the voting age: "Many citizens in our own country believe that they are entitled to assume greater responsibility for the destiny of our society. Such demands, in so far as they do not conflict with the general welfare, are the expression of a truly democratic ideal. They must be satisfied if our society is to attain its goals of peace and justice" (Speech from the Throne, 1969).

In lowering the voting age, Parliament became one of several legislative institutions in North America and Europe to bring younger citizens into the electorate. By 1969 seven Canadian provinces had already lowered the voting age, as had the United Kingdom. The remaining provinces and territories soon followed suit. In 1970 Germany established eighteen as the age for voting, and the United States adopted the same principle a year later. The general acceptance of the change in Canada was reflected in the parliamentary debates, in which there was virtually unanimous support for the legislation. In

keeping with the move to empower young Canadians, the age of political candidacy was lowered to eighteen at the same time. This move to
empower those between eighteen and twenty-one had its roots in the
civic unrest and student strikes in parts of Europe (especially France
and West Germany) in the late 1960s. As well there was a growing
sense among industrially advanced democracies of that time that the
youth of their countries were entitled to full electoral standing; that is,
to be able to vote and to run for public office.

The Charter and the Franchise

The Canadian electorate was further expanded following the adoption
of the Canadian Charter of Rights and Freedoms in 1982. According to
section 3 of the Charter, "Every citizen of Canada has the right to vote
in an election of members of the House of Commons or of a legislative
assembly and to be qualified for membership therein." This provision
opened the door to court challenges that eventually extended the right
to vote to groups of Canadians long denied the franchise. In the words
of Madam Justice Arbour: "The slow movement toward universal suffrage in Western democracies took an irreversible step forward in
Canada in 1982 by the enactment of section 3 of the Charter. I doubt
that anyone could now be deprived of the vote on the basis, not merely
symbolically but actually demonstrated, that he or she was not decent
or responsible" (*Sauvé v. Canada* 1992).

Successful court challenges based on the Charter extended the
franchise to federal judges and to the mentally disabled. In a 1988
case brought by two federal judges, the Federal Court of Canada commented that it was unfortunate that the issue had to be resolved in the
courts rather than by Parliament. That said, the court ruled that the
prohibition on judges voting clearly violated section 3 of the Charter.
The same reasoning applied to the exclusion of mentally challenged
Canadians in a 1988 case launched by the Canadian Disability Rights
Council. In light of these decisions and of the possibility that a successful

court challenge could be launched by expatriate Canadians, the Canada Elections Act was amended in the 1990s to extend the franchise to Canadian persons living abroad for up to five years who intend to return to Canada (*Muldoon v. Canada* 1988; *Canadian Disability Rights Council v. Canada* 1988).

Court challenges based on the Charter have also helped expand the franchise to prison inmates. The question of prisoners having a vote has been particularly contentious for governments at both the federal and provincial levels. Until late in 2002 when the Supreme Court of Canada finally resolved the issue, various jurisdictions had handled the question differently. Even before the Charter, the 1979 Quebec Elections Act gave the vote in Quebec to all inmates except for those serving time for violations of the province's Elections Act. In 1985 Newfoundland followed suit, as did Manitoba. At the federal level, in 1993, all inmates serving less then two years were granted the vote in response to a Supreme Court ruling that all prisoners holding Canadian citizenship should have the right to vote. However, when this legislation was successfully challenged in 1996, the vote was temporarily extended to all prison inmates until such time as the courts resolved the issue. That resolution came late in 2002 when, in a 5-4 decision, the Supreme Court of Canada struck down the section of the Canada Elections Act denying the right to vote to "every person who is imprisoned in a correctional institution serving a sentence of two years or more," which had been added by Parliament in 1993.

Writing for the majority in the 2002 case, the Supreme Court of Canada's chief justice rejected the contention that the vote should be denied to those who had committed serious crimes. The Crown had argued that there is a rational connection between respect for the law and the larger objective of promoting civic responsibility through the award of the franchise. The Court rejected that argument. Its reasoning is worth quoting at length for the meaning it attaches to section 3 of the Charter. In the words of the majority:

> Denying penitentiary inmates the right to vote is more likely
> to send messages that undermine respect for the law and

democracy than messages that enhance those values. The legitimacy of the law and the obligation to obey the law flow directly
from the right of every citizen to vote. To deny prisoners the
right to vote is to lose an important means of teaching them
democratic values and social responsibility. The government's
novel political theory that would permit elected representatives
to disenfranchise a segment of the population finds no place in
a democracy built upon principles of *inclusiveness, equality,*
and *citizen participation.* That not all self-proclaimed democracies adhere to this conclusion says little about what the Canadian vision of democracy embodied in the Charter permits.
Moreover, the argument that only those who respect the law
should participate in the political process cannot be accepted.
Denial of the right to vote on the basis of attributed moral
unworthiness is inconsistent with the respect for the dignity of
every person that lies at the heart of Canadian democracy and
the Charter (*Sauvé v. Canada* 2002, 4-5, emphasis added).

The American franchise laws with respect to prisoners' voting
rights (which vary among the fifty states for federal and state elections) speak to a major difference on that issue from Canada. In
Florida, which turned out to be the decisive state in the 2000 presidential election, some 450,000 current and former felons were disenfranchised at the time of the 2000 election. This amounted to 7 percent of
the state's total voting-age population. Florida, along with Texas and
four other states, bars former felons from ever voting again in the
state (Grose and Yoshinaka 2002, 20). This type of deliberate exclusion
of a segment of the larger citizenry is unimaginable by current Canadian standards.

What is important about the 2002 Sauvé decision is that the majority of the Court refused to accept, in the words of the four dissenting
justices, the proposition that "*responsible* citizenship ... is logically
related to whether or not a person engages in serious criminal activity." Instead, the majority pronounced that the right of every citizen to
vote "lies at the heart of Canadian democracy" and that "the idea that

certain classes of people are not morally fit or morally worthy to vote and to participate in the law-making process is ancient and obsolete" (*Sauvé v. Canada* 2002, 49, 19, and 37, emphasis in original). With this decision, which applies to the provinces and territories as well as to Parliament, the right to vote in Canada has been further expanded. Apart from age, there are now effectively no restrictions on voting for Canadian citizens resident in Canada.

The issue of discrimination on the basis of age has surfaced from time to time. A court challenge in 1994 based on the Charter argued that the franchise should be extended to include minors who had reached the age of twelve(!). In rejecting the challenge, the court concluded that "pragmatism dictates that reasonable restrictions such as age and mental capacity be imposed on the right to vote." It went on to argue that "the right to vote is subject to obvious exclusions such as those extending to minors" (*Reid v. Canada* 1994). The 1991 Royal Commission on Electoral Reform and Party Financing (the Lortie Commission) had considered recommending that the voting age be lowered to sixteen. Its concern was that restricting the franchise to citizens who are at least eighteen years of age was arbitrary and might constitute a possible infringement of sections 3 (the right to vote) and 15 (prohibiting discrimination based on age) of the Charter. After weighing the arguments, however, the Lortie Commission concluded that the voting age should remain at eighteen. It justified its decision on the grounds that under most statutes a person would not be considered an adult until that age. Applications for citizenship, marriage, and access to certain medical procedures were all cited by Lortie as examples in which people under eighteen required adult approval.

A Paradox

The current Canadian electoral system is a model of inclusiveness. But the history of twists and turns that the franchise has taken shows that has not always been the case. For many years after Confederation, federal and provincial governments showed little interest in extending the franchise beyond property-owning males. Moreover, governments did not hesitate to use the franchise for clearly partisan purposes. In so doing they acted with an arbitrary and self-interested zeal that would be considered unacceptable today by the courts and public opinion. The expanded franchise, now widened to include all parts of Canada's socially diverse adult citizenry, is here to stay. As matters currently stand almost all Canadians over the age of eighteen are eligible to vote, surely making Canada's widely inclusive franchise the envy of many around the world.

But a virtually universal franchise is no guarantee of high levels of voter turnout in elections. The reduced level of voter participation currently presents a serious issue to be addressed in the context of Canadian democracy. The statistics speak for themselves. In 1988, 75 percent of those on the electoral list voted. In 1993 the number slipped to 71 percent. In 1997 and 2000 it fell to 67 and 61 percent respectively. The 2000 election saw the lowest voter turnout in Canadian history.

To put this in comparative perspective, Richard Johnston notes that in 2000, of Canada's voting-age population (as distinct from registered electorate) "only 55 per cent ... turned out, hardly better than the 50 per cent [in the United States]" (Johnston 2001, 5). At the provincial level the trend has been similar. Although in three provinces turnout has increased marginally since 1980, in five provinces it has declined. Nowhere has the decline been greater than in Saskatchewan, where the share of the total eligible electorate slipped by 17 percentage points in the 1995 and 1999 elections from what it had been in the three previous elections. These figures put "Canada near the bottom of the industrialized-world turnout league tables ... Canada has never had a peculiarly high turnout, but the gradual decline from the 1960s to 1980s, followed by the precipitate drop in the 1990s, has taken us from the lower middle of the pack to near the very back" (Johnston 2001, 6).

The decline in voting in Canada and other Western democracies is more pronounced within certain groups. Education is a factor, with the more educated being more likely to vote. Marital status and mobility also affect voting. There is clear evidence that married people are more likely to vote than single people, and that citizens who have deep roots in a community are more likely to vote than those who move frequently (Teixeira 1987, 107-14). In North America and Europe age is the most important determinant of voting: older people are generally more likely to vote than younger ones. It is noteworthy that the decline in voter participation is most prevalent among those born after 1970. In the 2000 Canadian election, they were three times less likely to vote than baby boomers and seven times less likely to vote than pre-baby boomers. Among those who follow generation X, the decline in voting is especially acute among those with less education. This point was made effectively in a comparative study of two groups of voters in recent Canadian elections:

> Consider the situation of a thirty year old baby boomer in elections held before 1990. His/her predicted probability of voting is 80% if he/she has a university education and 64% if he/she has not completed secondary school, an important gap of 16 points. But compare the situation of those born in 1970 and who were aged thirty at the time of the 2000 election. Their predicted probability of voting is 66% if they have completed a university degree and only 37% if they have not completed their secondary education, a huge gap of 29 points (Blais et al. 2001, 6).

The decline in voting can be traced to many causes. They are considered more fully in another book in the Democratic Audit series (Gidengil et al. 2004), but it is fair to list a few of them so that we can better appreciate what almost certainly led to a decline in voter participation in the 1990s. By the late 1980s, Canadians had come to dislike and distrust Brian Mulroney, which in turn contributed to a more pronounced sense of dissatisfaction with the Canadian political system than had been evident for some time. The collapse of the Conservative vote in 1993; the subsequent fragmentation of the national party system and electoral dominance of the Liberals; the widespread public disaffection with federal and provincial politicians; the skepticism among many potential voters that their vote was "worth much" and that governments would deliver on their election promises once in office; the "decline of deference" to public authority that was detected in Canada in the 1990s; and the introduction in the mid-1990s of the permanent voters list for federal and several provincial elections: all of these can be seen as contributing in some measure to the fact that a smaller and smaller share of eligible voters took part in Canadian elections. In any case, the ever-wider net cast by the franchise laws to guarantee more Canadians the right to vote was, in itself, clearly no guarantee that electors would vote when the occasion presented itself.

Where Are We Now?

The franchise in Canada has been expanded greatly since Confederation. The early decades of Canada's suffrage history were marked more by who was excluded from voting than by who was included in the pool of potential electors. Race, property, gender, occupation, age, and province of residence were all used at one time or another to define a narrow, constricted electorate.

In the early twenty-first century it can be said that that is all behind us. In terms of both their federal and provincial franchise laws, Canadians can boast of a generous, inclusive set of requirements based solely on minimum age and citizenship. The current franchise standards have resulted from a mix of political motives, changing social values, international influences, and court-ordered norms defining electoral rights. Part of the credit for the widening of the franchise can also be given to social interest groups as varied as the Women's Suffrage Association, trade unions, the Women's Christian Temperance Union, progressive farm movements, and the Canadian Disability Rights Council. Their various successes speak to the responsiveness of policy makers and courts to organized calls for political reforms when the reformers come armed with a clear alternative to the status quo.

What remains to be done is unclear, in part because so much has been done over the past 135 years, and in part because the principal group of Canadians still denied the vote are those who have lived abroad for more than five years. The precise number of expatriate Canadians is unknown: estimates range from several hundred thousand to, possibly, a few million. The question raised by their exclusion from voting when they have been out of the country for more than five years is simple. Is the right to vote a right to be granted, with few exceptions, to those who reside in Canada, or is it a right that Canadians carry with them for an indefinite period of time regardless of where they happen to live in the world? Given the history of successful court challenges to voting restrictions since the adoption of the Charter, it is conceivable that a court challenge may at some point be forthcoming from aggrieved expatriate Canadians who seek to have the issue resolved in their favour. If they too were successful in their claim, Canada's already substantial electorate would become even larger.

Chapter 2

* Canada's franchise has become increasingly more inclusive, to the point that now almost every Canadian citizen is entitled to vote.

* As interpreted by the courts, the Charter of Rights and Freedoms ensures every citizen the right to vote.

* Electoral participation levels are declining.

FROM GERRYMANDERING TO INDEPENDENCE

TERRITORIALLY BASED DISTRICTS

3

As well as having been established in 1867 as a parliamentary democracy based on what is now generally called the Westminster model, Canada was created as a federal union. With the passage of time the combination of British parliamentarism and a variant of American federalism led to the growth of an officially bilingual, multicultural, geographically vast country with a relatively small and unevenly distributed population. Those constitutional, demographic, and territorial dimensions of contemporary Canada collectively prescribe the context within which electoral districts are constructed.

The means whereby electoral district boundaries are designed have been fundamentally reformed since Confederation. Under the Constitution Parliament is required to redistribute its electoral constituencies (or "ridings" as Canadians prefer to call them) following every decennial census. This process has two stages. Because the country is federal in structure the first part of the redistribution process requires an allocation of the Commons' districts amongst the provinces and territories. The second stage involves the actual design of the ridings themselves within each of the provinces. (The three territories are so sparsely populated that they receive only one district each.)

Why is the drawing of constituency boundaries important to a democratic audit of Canada's electoral regime? The answer, which expands somewhat on the audit's principal criteria of participation, responsiveness, and inclusiveness, is threefold. First, at the level of institutional process or procedure, we can judge how *fair* the periodic exercise of boundary readjustments is. By comparing the process in place at the time of Confederation with the current one we can determine what has changed and whether the changes have been for the better. If the procedural reforms to the drawing of constituency boundaries carried out over the past 135 years were in the direction of enabling greater public participation and inclusiveness in the process and of ensuring institutional responsiveness to public input, we can say that the process has become more democratic.

Second, we should assess the impact that the methods of redistribution and the outcomes of boundary readjustments have on Canada's notion of voter *equality*. To determine that, we need to consider the "value" of one person's vote in relation to another's and the extent to which the outcome of the process ensures a more or less equitable treatment of citizens for the purposes of electing their representatives. In this respect the critical questions are how similar the population sizes of the electoral districts are and, in a federal state such as Canada, whether representational considerations other than population suitably enter into the redistribution process.

Third, as the aggregation of interests in territorially defined districts ultimately affects *representation* in Parliament, legislatures, cabinets, and public policy, the system's capacity to ensure effective representation must also be considered. Citizen representation and the formulation of public policy are at the heart of a democratic electoral process. Thus the construction of the territorially defined districts from which the elected representatives are chosen is important.

From Gerrymanders to the Eve of Reform

In the past, members of Parliament carried out both stages of the redistribution exercise themselves. This clearly left the process open to widespread criticism, for the MPs' interests were most immediately affected by the configuration of the districts they were designing. Each decennial redistribution led, ultimately, to a redistribution act passed by Parliament, which effectively meant that the potential for political trade-offs amongst the parties, leaders, and members was considerable. The atmosphere was invariably highly charged, partisan, and full of electoral implications for both government and opposition members.

Nine federal decennial redistributions were carried out between 1872 and 1952 under these conditions. Without exception each was carefully managed by the government of the day, whether Conservative or Liberal, in its own interest. The great majority of the redistributions, especially the thinly disguised gerrymander of 1882, were partisan and blatantly self-serving affairs. A few, notably the 1952 exercise, were the work of a government-dominated parliamentary committee on which all parties in the House sought and gained certain favours through a series of political trade-offs. In none of the nine boundary readjustments was the public invited to participate, nor was it formally consulted. For the better part of a century Canada's boundary readjustments were totally partisan, in-house exercises which, by design, excluded the public.

Every redistribution was subjected to editorial and public criticism at the time and led opposition parties, not unexpectedly, to pledge to end the practice of partisan gerrymandering if they won office. But no change in the redistribution system ever followed a change in government. Newly elected parties invariably found compelling reasons to keep their hands on the process. The history of promised but subsequently undelivered reforms to Canada's electoral boundary readjustment process was long and not particularly honourable. As one MP described it in a Commons debate in 1939, the process of readjusting electoral boundaries in Canada amounted to "an unseemly, undignified and utterly confusing scramble for personal [and] political advantage" (House of Commons 1939, 1808).

At the provincial level, electoral boundary readjustments suffered a worse fate. Without constitutional requirements similar to those spelled out for the Parliament of Canada, the provinces were under no obligation to readjust the boundaries of their legislative assemblies at regular intervals. As a consequence redistributions in a province, if they were held at all, were often decades apart. As populations inevitably shifted, the long delays between redistributions had the effect of increasing the disparity among the populations of provincial constituencies.

When they did occur, redistributions were invariably under the control of the governing party and were frequently introduced in the legislature without prior consultation with the opposition parties. Biases against urban and in favour of rural voters were common to all provinces, varying only in the degree of their discrimination. Provincial politicians calling for reform of the redistribution system were found exclusively on the opposition benches, and editorialists, academics, and interested members of the general public urging the adoption of nonpartisan boundary readjustment commissions received no support from the governing elites.

Quebec, admittedly an extreme case even by Canadian provincial redistribution standards, exemplified the problems faced at the provincial level. The province made no regular boundary readjustments of its electoral districts. Instead the government simply added more districts or split existing ones into two or three parts as the need arose (and the government's political instincts suggested). Constituencies were left largely unchanged from when they were first designed in 1853 at the close of the seigneurial era.

By 1960 the effects of more than a century of deliberate malapportionment of Quebec's constituencies were obvious. Barely one-third of the provincial assembly's districts fell within 15 percent of the average district population size. The range in terms of population told a similar story: the three smallest ridings (all rural) contained an average of 6,800 voters each, whereas the three largest (all in Montreal suburbs) averaged 108,000 voters each. Measured by the Dauer-Kelsay index (a then fashionable, but crude, way of gauging inequality), the smallest percentage of the entire population theoretically needed to elect a majority of the assembly fell from 39 percent in 1861 to 26 percent a century later.

In other words, one-quarter of the Quebec electorate could, at least in theory, elect a majority of the assembly's members. In that respect Quebec was *more* malapportioned, and voters in that province were more unequally distributed among their ridings, than was the case in the state of Tennessee at roughly the same time (1962) when the United States Supreme Court issued its historic *Baker* v. *Carr* decision. That decision, which relied on an application of the Dauer-Kelsay index, forced Tennessee and, eventually, all other states to undertake regular redistricting. It ushered in the principle of "one person, one vote" that is now central to the construction of congressional and state districts in the United States.

The Quebec example is instructive about democracy in that province in the late 1950s and early 1960s. Voters differed mightily in their ability to affect electoral outcomes. They might have participated in equal numbers throughout the province, but that mattered far less than where they lived. Depending upon the location of the constituencies in which they were cast, votes carried differential weights in determining an election's outcome. With few exceptions, voters in urban and suburban districts had far less electoral clout than voters in rural districts. Voters in the province's three smallest ridings had, effectively, sixteen times more weight in electing a legislative member than voters in the three largest ridings (108,000 ÷ 6,800 = 16). Residents of rural Quebec were thus vastly overrepresented in the national assembly compared with those who lived in or around the large metropolitan areas. The location of constituencies had a telling impact on the complexion of the legislature, the composition of the government and, ultimately, on public policy. Conservative, parochial, and tilted in the direction of rural, agricultural interests, Quebec's legislature in the late 1950s scarcely constituted a representative slice of the newly emerging urban, more secular, and more liberal Quebec society.

In varying degrees, Quebec's distribution of legislative districts in the mid-twentieth century was found in the other provinces and at the federal level as well. Indeed, federalism complicated an already complicated issue by further skewing the differences in populations among the Commons' constituencies. As we will see in the next section, the allocation of constituencies among the provinces has played a big part in determining the degree of inequality among the districts. Suffice it to note here that in the last federal election before the replacement of government-controlled redistributions with independent boundary commissions, federal seats varied considerably in size. The extremes in the 1965 federal election were York-Scarborough in Ontario with 267,252 residents and Iles-de-la-Madeleine in Quebec with 12,479 residents. Such manifestly unequal distribution of voters among federal ridings added fuel to the already heated debate about the need to reform Canada's electoral boundary process.

Allocating Constituencies to the Provinces

Before considering the reforms adopted at both the federal and provincial levels to address the inequality of riding population sizes and to end the practice of gerrymandering by elected members, it is necessary to explain the factors that enter into the allocation of Commons seats among the provinces at the outset of each decennial redistribution. The number of seats awarded a province has never conformed strictly to a province's share of the Canadian population. Instead, various guarantees have been put in place over the years to placate those provinces that had either a declining population or a population that was growing more slowly than the national rate. The guarantees were designed to ensure that provinces did not lose the number of seats they would have lost otherwise or, alternatively, to assure them of a fixed minimum number of federal constituencies in perpetuity. Two essential principles govern the allocation of seats:

1   The "senatorial floor" clause adopted by way of a 1915 constitu-
    tional amendment stipulates that no province will ever have
    fewer MPs than it has members of the Senate.

2   The "grandfather clause" law of 1985 ensures that no province
    will be granted fewer Commons seats than it had in 1976 or in the
    33rd Parliament (1984-8), whichever is fewer.

The effect of these provisions is shown in Table 3.1, which gives the
breakdown of Commons seats by provinces for the post-2001 census
redistribution. Together the two provisions mean that seven of the ten
provinces are, as it were, frozen in time. Prince Edward Island has
been best served by the redistribution formula. It has been protected
for a longer period and owes a greater share of its Commons seats to
the application of the constitutionally entrenched senatorial guarantee than any other province. Since the 1915 adoption of the senatorial
floor for provincial representation in the Commons, PEI has remained
at four seats even though, as Table 3.1 shows, if the province were
awarded parliamentary districts only on the basis of its population it
would send only one MP to Ottawa.

The senatorial and grandfather clauses work to the benefit of those
provinces with static or declining populations and against those
whose populations have grown faster over the preceding decade than
the national average. For the past three decades the populations of
Ontario, Alberta, and British Columbia have grown faster than the
national average rate. Therefore the remaining seven provinces now
have more Commons seats than their populations warrant. For the
redistribution based on the 2001 census, the two guarantees added 27
seats to a Commons that would otherwise be in the order of 281 or 282
members (see the "Special Clauses" column of Table 3.1).

Strictly from the standpoint of the "value" of each citizen's vote, the
differential treatment of provinces contributes substantially to the
variations in average constituency size across the country. In the post-
2001 redistribution the provincial averages for seats vary from 33,824
in Prince Edward Island to 108,548 in British Columbia. In a straight

Table 3.1

Post-2001 redistribution of parliamentary seats

Province or territory	Number of seats established in 1976 and constituting 33rd Parliament[1]	Population 2001	Calculations				Provincial quotient
			National quotient (rounded)[2]	Rounded result	Special clauses[3]	Total	
Newfoundland	7	512,930	107,220	5	2	7	73,276
Prince Edward Island	4	135,294	107,220	1	3	4	33,824
Nova Scotia	11	908,007	107,220	8	3	11	82,546
New Brunswick	10	729,498	107,220	7	3	10	72,950
Quebec	75	7,237,479	107,220	68	7	75	96,500
Ontario	95	11,410,046	107,220	106	–	106	107,642
Manitoba	14	1,119,583	107,220	10	4	14	79,970
Saskatchewan	14	978,933	107,220	9	5	14	69,924
Alberta	21	2,974,807	107,220	28	–	28	106,243
British Columbia	28	3,907,738	107,220	36	–	36	108,548
Provincial total	279	29,914,315	–	278	27	305	–
Northwest Territories	1	37,360	–	1	–	1	–
Nunavut	1	26,745	–	1	–	1	–
Yukon Territory	1	28,674	–	1	–	1	–
Total	282	30,007,094	–	281	27	308	–

Notes

1 Assign one seat each to the Yukon, Northwest Territories, and Nunavut.
2 Use 279 seats and population of provinces to establish national quotient (29,914,315 ÷ 279 = 107,220).
3 Add seats to provinces pursuant to the senatorial floor guarantee in the Constitution and the grandfather clause.

comparison of the two provinces the vote of a Prince Edward Islander could be said to be "worth" a little more than three times that of a British Columbian. In other words, in the first decade of the twenty-first century it will take three times the number of British Columbians as Prince Edward Islanders to elect a single MP (see "Provincial Quotient" column of Table 3.1). For BC residents (as for those in Alberta and Ontario) it would be difficult to accept any claim that for the purposes of calculating their electoral worth they were being treated the same as Canadians in other provinces.

But there is another side to the issue. Provincial entitlement to Commons seats is of vital importance to executive governance at the federal level. There has long been an established link in Canada between membership in the cabinet and the country's federal structure. That link bears crucially on the distribution of Commons seats among the provinces and helps to account for the reluctance of the smaller provinces and Quebec to accept a formula that would reduce their parliamentary representation. We will see in the conclusion to this chapter that any attempt to cut back on provincial entitlement to Commons seats could be expected to meet with stiff opposition from seven of the ten provinces because of the possibly negative consequences on their presence in the federal cabinet.

Designing Districts

Once the first stage of the decennial redistribution exercise has been completed and the provinces have been assigned their seats, an independent electoral boundary readjustment commission is established in each province. The theory behind this is that local commissioners are more likely to be familiar with the local communities, the history, the population shifts, and the geography of a province than would a single national commission charged with designing all three hundred or so constituencies across the country. Insofar as locally knowledgeable commissioners are preferred to a single set of officials applying standards uniformly across the country, the federal boundary re-adjustment process has been established with responsiveness to provincially defined interests in mind. This is very much in keeping with the social, economic, and territorial variations one expects to be nurtured and protected by a federal system of government.

The provincial composition of the ten federal commissions has given credibility to the electoral boundaries process. Each of the com-missions is chaired by a judge appointed by the chief justice of the province from one of the district or superior courts of the province. The two remaining members of the commission are named by the speaker of the Commons, sometimes on the recommendation of the chief electoral officer of Canada. These members are generally politi-cal scientists (an average of twelve of the twenty commissioners named to the redistributions following the 1991 and 2001 censuses were political scientists), other university-based social scientists, provincial election officials, and practising and university lawyers. Occasionally the speaker's choice of committee members has prompted charges of political partisanship. But such charges have been rare and the maps produced by the commissions have never shown any evidence of having been constructed with the deliberate objective of favouring one party over the others.

Obviously, as occupational categories go, social scientists, provin-cial election officials, and lawyers are not typical of the general popu-lation. But their overwhelming presence on the commissions speaks to a fundamental principle underlying the process. Quite deliberately, federal boundary readjustment commissions are not constructed with large memberships "representing" various occupational or demo-graphic segments of a province's population. Rather, they are com-posed of a small number of individuals knowledgeable about a province's various communities of interest, its social and economic centres, geography, and political history. Canadian political scientists, in particular, have paid increasing attention to questions of represen-tation, communities of interest, shifts in population, and electoral democracy over the past couple of decades. The body of popular and academic literature on constituency redistricting produced by political scientists in the 1980s and 1990s was impressive, and university course offerings now pay greater attention to issues germane to electoral boundaries and constituency readjustments than in the past. Lawyers and former and present provincial election officials are also well positioned to reflect on the wisdom of alternative configurations of district boundaries.

Members of the judiciary are attractive as chairs of commissions. Judges are not elected in Canada, and although many have played some role in partisan politics prior to their appointment to the bench, they have nonetheless been widely seen to fill judicial positions with independence and nonpartisanship. Their skills, in a sense, complement those of the other members of their commission. Judges are not students of electoral districting like electoral officials or some political scientists. But judges are accustomed to listening to competing arguments, adjudicating disputes, and handing down decisions. Theirs is a skill of accommodating differences, of balancing competing interests, and of attempting to determine what is fair and right within the terms of the law. As decision makers they are accustomed to having their decisions satisfy some, dissatisfy others, and possibly be overturned on appeal. Fairness, credibility, and decisiveness are important attributes for any chair to have when, as with electoral boundary commissions, the position calls for open consultation and hearings with the public about the possible design of the maps.

Canada Adopts Independent Boundary Commissions

The province of Manitoba was the first Canadian jurisdiction, in 1955, to replace government-dominated, partisan redistributions with arm's-length, nonpartisan commissions charged with redefining constituency boundaries. In fact, this history provides an object lesson about the democratizing potential inherent in federalism. A federal system is like a giant test tube for institutional role modelling, which is to say that if an innovative institution or policy is successful in one jurisdiction it eventually makes its way elsewhere. Dozens of public policies in Canada, from medicare to snowmobile regulations, originated in a single jurisdiction before being embraced by others.

A confluence of three political developments set the stage for all-party approval in Manitoba of legislation establishing independent electoral boundary commissions. These were glaring voter inequities resulting from a history of government-controlled redistributions; reform-oriented and innovative opposition parties, soon joined by the premier, pushing a novel idea; and a measure of public and political dissatisfaction with the proportional representation and **alternative vote (AV)** electoral systems then used for provincial elections.

During the first half of the twentieth century successive governments in Manitoba had consciously sought to overrepresent rural areas in the provincial legislature. Following the government-controlled redistribution of 1949 (the first seat reallocation in twenty-nine years), the gross disparity between urban and rural Manitobans was abundantly clear: the province's 228,280 urban voters were represented by seventeen members in the legislature and the 224,083 voters in rural Manitoba by forty members. Urban residents, backed by opposition members, called for "fair representation," by which they not only meant relatively equal district populations but also an end to government-controlled redistributions that were widely seen as open to abuse. Coinciding with these events was the growing hostility to **single transferable vote (STV)** elections for selecting provincial MLAs from Winnipeg.

This last point sheds light on a feature of the debate over electoral systems that is often overlooked and that we will return to in a later chapter. Faraway pastures look greener in electoral reform as well as in the countryside. Manitoba had adopted STV for Winnipeg and AV for the remainder of the province at the close of the First World War in order to "open up" the system of electing the legislative assembly. The stated goal was to make the legislature "more representative and democratic," and to ensure that "fairer" conversion of votes into seats took place. But after more than thirty years of coalition governments,

Manitoba politicians, the media, and much of the public saw STV (AV had by then been abandoned) as the main barrier to single-party majority government. In Winnipeg the criticisms levelled at the proportional representation scheme as well as the calls for a more openly competitive party system proved to be particularly strong (Courtney 2001, ch. 3).

The city's method of electing MLAs from multimember ridings had fallen into disrepute for three principal reasons. There was marked inequality of populations among the ridings; fierce and often destructive fights took place among candidates of the same party for election within ridings; and the widespread impression had been created that multimember districts did not encourage the close contacts between elected members and voters that single-member districts were claimed to foster. The first problem had nothing to do with the electoral system per se, for equal distribution of voters can as easily take place among multimember constituencies as single-member ones. The second and third criticisms are often levelled at electoral systems with multimember districts. The arguments over which electoral system was best for the province had gone full circle in thirty-five years.

The legislative committee that designed Manitoba's independent electoral boundaries act relied heavily on the Australian model of redistributing its parliamentary seats. Australia shared much in common with Canada in 1955. It was a geographically large federal country with a parliamentary system, it had two large urban centres, and much of its hinterland was sparsely settled. The Manitoba committee's fundamental premise was that "representation by population should be the basis of electoral divisions," but that population should not be the only factor to be considered when seats were designed. Equally important were "community or diversity of interest, means of communication and physical features." Australian experience had demonstrated, the committee reasoned, that all of these factors could be successfully brought into the boundary readjustment exercise. Australia also showed that the entire process could be handled by small nonpartisan commissions made up of judges, election officials, and the like, to remove the possibility of gerrymandering.

Manitoba's success in establishing a process whereby district boundaries would be regularly redesigned by a nonpartisan body was adopted within a decade by Parliament for federal ridings. From there the idea spread to the province of Quebec. Over the course of the next twenty-five years all the remaining provinces and the three territories adopted some variant of either the Manitoba or the federal scheme. The "demonstration effect" of federalism held true for the establishment of independent electoral boundary commissions across Canada.

Elements of Federal and Provincial Boundary Readjustment Schemes

Ottawa's Electoral Boundaries Readjustment Act (adopted in 1964) set out the five basic elements of the federal exercise:

1 A separate three-member commission for each of the ten provinces was to be appointed by Order-in-Council (the cabinet) on recommendation of the speaker of the House and the chief justice of each province.

2 No constituency's population could vary by more than 25 percent above or below the provincial electoral quotient (a province's population divided by its number of seats) unless (as was added in 1985) there were "exceptional circumstances."

3 The population of each electoral district was to correspond "as nearly as may be" to the province's electoral quotient. Nonetheless the commissions were to consider the following in determining district boundaries: the community of interest or community of identity in, or the historical pattern of, an electoral district; and a manageable geographic size for districts in sparsely populated, rural, or northern regions of a province.

4 There was to be an opportunity for the public to present written briefs and to make representations at public meetings

called by the commission about the maps first proposed by the commission.

5 There was to be an opportunity for MPs to voice their concerns about the proposed maps once formal objections to a commission's work had been filed with the speaker of the House by any ten members. The debate precipitated by the objections would, with the maps as originally proposed, be forwarded to the commission for its consideration. The decision of the commission would then be final.

These five elements of electoral boundary readjustments have recast Canada's redistribution process. Determining the size and shape of electoral districts is no longer the exclusive preserve of the politicians. The independence of the commissioners is one of the fundamental pillars on which the new process has been built. The opportunity for public participation in the redistribution process stands as another of the pillars. A third, as we will see, rests on the willingness of commissions over the past forty years to construct districts that are more equal in population than was previously the case. A fourth pillar, critical to success in a diverse federal system such as Canada's, has been the acceptance of differences based on communities of interest and geographic size. Together these four pillars have democratized one of the essential building blocks of Canada's electoral system. Details of the various provincial systems vary, but most of their fundamental aspects closely approximate the federal legislation, which, in turn, was styled on Manitoba's statute.

The principles on which seats are to be constructed are similar, in some respects identical, in the federal and provincial legislation. "Community of interest" remains the term common to almost all jurisdictions, although the phrase is left largely undefined. Different commissions, and even successive commissions within the same jurisdiction, can therefore attach different meanings to the term. As a rule commissions are guided by what they determine to be the important socioeconomic variables of a community, the geography of a region and, in the words of Quebec's legislation, "population density, the relative growth rate of the population, the accessibility, area or shape of the region, the natural local boundaries and the limits of municipalities" (Statutes of Quebec 1979, ss. 7 and 8). Commissions at both the federal and provincial levels have been mindful of the need to construct their districts with familiar administrative structures (health or education districts, rural municipalities, counties, and the like) as the basis of their interpretation of territorially defined communities of interest.

No jurisdiction issues explicit instructions to commissions to construct districts according to racial, ethnic, linguistic, or religious characteristics. In some areas of the country (particularly the large metropolitan centres) it would be difficult for commissions to construct seats that did not capture in some way the territorial concentration of groups with such common ties. The anglophone minorities in Montreal, the Italian, Chinese, and Greek communities of Toronto, and the Chinese and Sikh communities of Vancouver are now all sizable enough to constitute either an absolute majority or a substantial part of some districts.

The only commissions at either the federal or provincial level to have made a conscious effort to construct districts with targeted minority populations as the principal justification for a particular set of boundaries were those of the province of Nova Scotia in their two most recent redistributions. The commissions' terms of reference included no maximum or minimum population limits for constituency size, but they did require consideration of "minority representation" in constructing seats. To that end the commissions were instructed in 1992 to "seek out the advice, support and cooperation of, in particular, representatives of the Black, Native, and Acadian communities of the Province" (Nova Scotia Electoral Boundaries Commission 1992, 13). Each of these three communities has a relatively small share of Nova Scotia's population, ranging from an estimated 1 percent for the Natives to 5 percent for the Acadians. In spite of their small numbers, all have deep roots in the province.

The Nova Scotia commissions tried to create a more inclusive and responsive provincial legislative assembly. For example, in 1992 the Nova Scotia commissioners decided to ensure a degree of "minority representation" in the fifty-two-seat legislature by fashioning what they called "protected constituencies." This was a term coined to describe districts created around "minority group population concentration" (Nova Scotia Electoral Boundaries Commission 1992, 13). Three of the four protected seats had populations well below the provincial average. In only two Acadian seats did the minority constitute a majority of the population. The protected constituencies were justified on grounds of wanting to "encourage, but not guarantee" the election of three Acadians and one Black to the legislature. Indeed, in the following provincial election Acadians captured the three specially constructed seats, and the carefully crafted Halifax riding elected the first black member of the provincial assembly in its nearly 250-year history. No agreement could be reached with Nova Scotia's Native community to add a fifty-third seat to the legislature reserved for a Native member to be elected by Nova Scotia Natives across the province.

The Courts and Redistribution

Section 3 of the Canadian Charter of Rights and Freedoms guarantees every citizen of Canada "the right to vote." To date the only section 3 challenge heard by the Supreme Court of Canada came in 1991 in what has become commonly referred to as the *Carter* decision. Roger Carter, QC, presented the case for the Society for the Advancement of Voter Equality (SAVE) seeking the Court's opinion on the constitutional validity of Saskatchewan's recently adopted electoral boundaries. SAVE had been formed in response to the constituency maps prepared under the province's Representation Act, 1989. That act empowered Saskatchewan's three-member independent commission to create seats in all but the northern part of the province with tolerance limits of ±25 percent of the electoral quotient determined after the population of the two northern seats had been removed from the provincial population. It made a further distinction among the seats in the southern part of the province by dividing them into rural and urban categories. SAVE contended that the seats created as a consequence of the legislation violated the principle of equality of the vote.

To the Supreme Court the basic question was "whether the variances and distribution reflected in the constituencies themselves violate[d] the Charter guarantee of the right to vote." They found that they did not. The majority's line of reasoning (in a 6-3 decision) was that in enshrining the right to vote in the written Constitution, the framers of the Charter had never intended to adopt the "American model" of "voter parity," or "one person, one vote." According to the Court, Canada's more pragmatic, pluralist, and group-based notions of "effective representation" could be traced back to 1867. The decision held that the right to vote guaranteed by the Charter was "not equality of voting power per se but the right to 'effective representation.'" In the words of Madam Justice McLachlin, "effective representation is at the heart of the right to vote." Recognizing that absolute equality of voting power is impossible (because "voters die, voters move"), the Court accepted "relative parity of voting power" as the principal condition underlying effective representation (*Reference re: Provincial Election Boundaries* 1991, 7, 13-14, 16).

The Court was clear about not countenancing the "dilution" of one citizen's vote relative to another's. Deviations from strict parity of voters would be permitted only when an alternative design was impossible for practical reasons, when they could be "justified on the ground that they contribute to better government" of the population, or when they could be justified by population growth projections. Relative equality of voter power could also be "undesirable" if it detracted from the primary goal of effective representation: "Factors like geography, community history, community interests and minority representation may need to be taken into account to ensure that our legislative assemblies effectively represent the diversity of our social mosaic. These are but examples of considerations that may justify departure from absolute voter parity in the pursuit of more effective representation; the list is not closed" (*Reference re: Provincial Election Boundaries* 1991, 7, 13-14, 16).

The critical contribution to the doctrine of electoral representation that the majority opinion of the Supreme Court made in Carter was fourfold. First, it eschewed American egalitarianism as the model for constructing electoral districts in Canada. Second, it validated the proposition that the purpose of the right to vote in the Charter is the right to effective representation, not to equality of voting power. Third, it established relative, not absolute, parity of voting power as the primary condition of effective representation. And fourth, it allowed for deviations from strict voter equality on grounds of projected population changes, practical impossibility due to the geographic size or shape of a riding, or the provision of more effective representation.

The Court's interpretation of section 3 as guaranteeing the right to effective representation has enabled federal and provincial jurisdictions to construct their legislation and the principles behind district redistributions in strikingly different ways. Nova Scotia has no legislated limits on the size of the districts its commission can create, whereas Saskatchewan modified its law to ensure that all but the two northern seats would be within a 5 percent limit of the mean population of the south. Both provinces justified these quite contradictory changes in terms of effective representation. The concept also served as the leading justification in Nova Scotia for the creation of the black and Acadian minority seats for election to the provincial assembly (Nova Scotia Electoral Boundaries Commission 1992). However, minority groups elsewhere have not seized on it as grounds for pushing for some equivalent measure of representation in the construction of electoral districts.

Aboriginal Electoral Districts

In recent years the idea of constructing one or more electoral districts containing a concentrated, socially identified group has received favourable attention from opinion leaders. Nova Scotia has been the most proactive of the provinces on this front. As we have seen, the province has turned to "affirmative gerrymandering" (as the practice is called in the United States, where it was first used) to enhance the likelihood that members of the black and Acadian minority populations would win seats in the legislature. The rationale for creating districts with concentrated minority populations is that certain racially or linguistically defined groups have been historically disadvantaged in electing assembly members. They deserve, so the argument goes, a deliberate or positive action on the state's part to promote their legislative presence.

No group has a more compelling case as a historically disadvantaged minority than Canada's Aboriginal population. With approximately 3.5 percent of the total Canadian population, Aboriginals have never come close to sending a proportionate number of elected members to Parliament or the provincial legislatures. The number of Aboriginal candidates for public office at all levels has been small, as has the number of Aboriginals who have voted. Those who favour specially constructed districts claim that with "their own" candidates running for office and serving as the elected members, Native voters will take greater interest in federal and provincial politics. That increased interest, they argue, is likely to improve the Aboriginal participation rates in elections.

The Lortie Commission stands out as the pre-eminent proponent of Aboriginal electoral districts (AEDs). Its 1991 report to the federal government strongly supported the notion of specially constructed Aboriginal seats for Parliament, maintaining that AEDs "would build upon the Canadian tradition of accommodating both individual and collective rights" (RCERPF 1991a, 178). Lortie offered four reasons in support of the proposal: the unique constitutional status of Aboriginals dating back to the Royal Proclamation of 1763; the expressed desire of Aboriginal peoples to preserve their separate identity; the special responsibilities of Parliament to legislate under section 91(24) of the Constitution Act, 1867; and the opportunity AEDs presented to promote political equality by ensuring, in keeping with *Carter*, effective parliamentary representation for Aboriginals.

The commission recommended that up to eight Aboriginal districts be established in Canada. An AED would be awarded to a province when the number of voters on a specially maintained Aboriginal register met a minimum requirement of 85 percent of the per seat electoral quotient for that province. Aboriginals would have the right to choose whether or not to register on the Aboriginal voters register. Those who did not opt for inclusion on the registry would be entitled to vote in the regular manner in the constituency in which they lived. Given the distribution of the Native population in Canada, the Lortie plan could mean one AED for each of Quebec, Manitoba, Saskatchewan, and Alberta, two in Ontario, and one or two in British Columbia. Additional AEDs would be established in a province when the growth in the Aboriginals' share of the province's total population warranted it. The Aboriginal seats awarded a province would not be additional, but would come out of its allocation as determined by the formula outlined in Table 3.1.

At one level, Lortie saw the issue as a *numerical* challenge – that is, how to increase the number of Aboriginal representatives and improve upon the dismal record of the past. But in a more profound way the argument presented by the royal commission was also a *representational* one. It signalled acceptance of the notion of deliberately mirroring a particular part of society in Parliament. This use of the concept of effective representation drew on *Carter* and on the commission's conclusion that Aboriginal people are "not simply one among many communities of interest." Rather, according to Lortie, they are "unique and [enjoy a] special status" (RCERPF 1991a, 173).

The construction that has long been given to the concept of "community of interest" in electoral districting in Canada derives directly from the single-member district, simple plurality voting system that has been used, with few exceptions, at both levels of government since Confederation. It is a system rooted in place, in a territorially defined area. Constituencies are by definition bounded areas, and are often

territorially small ones at that. The task as set forth in electoral boundary legislation since the 1950s has been to ensure that commissions
are mindful of the sociodemographic and economic variables of a
region as they go about designing their maps, and that they respect
those "communities" and their "interests" to the extent possible by
placing them within appropriately drawn boundaries.

Carter offered a way to grant special representational treatment to
a fragmented, relatively small community that had ample reason to
complain about its past treatment and about its current economic and
social plight. Aboriginal people do not constitute a community of
interest in the conventional sense of being relatively compact and territorially bounded. But there is a difficulty in identifying Aboriginal
Canadians as having clearly defined non-territorially bounded communities of interest. It has been pointed out that "the diversity of Aboriginal peoples is far deeper and more complex than the categories of
'Indian,' 'Inuit' and 'Métis.' There are status and non-status Indians,
urban and rural dwellers, a diversity of tribes, nations and linguistic
groups, treaty and non-treaty Indians, and men and women. The interests of many of these groups overlap but also diverge in significant
ways" (Schouls 1996, 743-4).

As it transpired, AEDs have become little more than an academic
question. The 1992 Charlottetown Accord called for guaranteed Aboriginal representation in the Senate and supported further discussions on "the issue of Aboriginal representation" in the Commons. But
the Accord's rejection in a countrywide referendum brought that particular proposal to an abrupt end. More critically, with the release of
the report of the Royal Commission on Aboriginal Peoples in 1996, the
question of Aboriginal representation moved well beyond a guaranteed presence for Aboriginals in the Commons. That commission recommended a radically different proposal: an Aboriginal parliament,
elected by Aboriginal nations or peoples, would constitute a third
chamber of Parliament alongside the Senate and the Commons. As
with AEDs, no action had been taken to implement this idea at the
beginning of the new millennium.

A recent attempt to implement a variant of AEDs came in a proposal floated by the New Brunswick federal electoral boundaries commission following the 2001 census. For the first time in Canadian history it designated one of the province's federal districts (Miramichi, with a population of 67,000) as a seat into which all fifteen Indian reserves in New Brunswick, irrespective of their location, would be grouped for electoral purposes. The estimated 11,000 to 12,000 residents of the province's reserves are dispersed around the province. Under the plan they would be linked to one another and to a single MP in a new and different fashion: racial ancestry would trump geography. The commission justified its call for the creation of a noncontiguous seat on the grounds that New Brunswick Aboriginals would no longer be "fragmented" in their representation in Ottawa. Instead, the commission asserted, reserve Indians would gain representational strength from having one elected member clearly responsible for speaking for their interests.

The proposal, as novel as it was, was rejected by the province's Aboriginals and dropped from the redistribution commission's final report. Most Native leaders called for its rejection on the grounds that it was better to keep the province's reserves within the federal riding that territorially encompassed them. That way Natives would be able to seek the services of several different MPs, possibly from more than one political party, when they sought representation in Ottawa. The chiefs' rejection of the proposal for a single noncontiguous seat also resulted from their strongly held view that they could, in their words, "wield far more influence ... by holding the balance of power in a number of closely contested ridings" (N.B. Native chiefs 2002).

Public Participation

Federal and provincial redistribution commissions are required to hold public hearings in various centres around their province and to provide members of the general public with the opportunity to make written or oral presentations prior to the production of any final constituency maps. Provincial commissions in British Columbia hold two rounds of public consultations; in other jurisdictions a single public consultative stage follows the publication of the commission's preliminary maps. Members of Parliament and of the provincial assemblies are also entitled to meet with their respective commissions at the public hearing stage and, in some jurisdictions, to record their objections to the proposals in committee or on the floor of their assembly. What is critical to the independence of the commissioners is that they are under no obligation to accept any of the opinions expressed to them by the public or the elected members.

One of the aims of the federal Electoral Boundaries Readjustment Act and of similar provincial statutes was to increase the public's awareness of and involvement in the redistribution process. Exact attendance numbers and participation rates have not always been recorded or published, so it is impossible to know precisely how many individuals have taken advantage of the widely publicized invitation to the public to attend a hearing and present a brief or testify before a commission. The available data show that the number of participants and briefs presented to commissions has never been large. Commissions in the bigger provinces rarely hear from more than a few hundred individuals, and in the smaller provinces sometimes no more than a few dozen.

It is clear as well that the numbers fluctuate from one boundary readjustment to another and from one area within a province to another according to the degree of public concern about the possible impact of the proposals on a particular region or riding. When citizens are sufficiently concerned about the implications of a set of boundary proposals for their community or about the possible loss of "their" legislative seat, a number will mobilize to argue against the proposal before the commission. When, on the other hand, the proposals do not raise any red flags in a locality, the commissioners find little public interest in their work. In other words, at least some citizens will respond to commission proposals only when they are seen as crucial to a local interest, community, or neighbourhood. Public responsiveness is issue-driven.

The participation rate in the public hearing stage of two recent federal redistributions demonstrates that the public has yet to become informed about or involved in the process of electoral boundary readjustments. The number of public submissions to all ten federal commissions came to 928 in the 1980s and 641 in the 1990s (Courtney 2001, 134). For the overwhelming majority of Canadians the design and total population of their federal and provincial ridings are unimportant, which perhaps best explains the general indifference to these matters. When there has been participation in a commission's hearing it has come almost invariably from mayors, councillors, and other elected officials, defeated candidates, and constituency party executives taking advantage of the opportunity to express their opinions about the proposed district boundaries. These intervenors cannot be considered the "general public" in the sense of an engaged citizenry. Their participation is prompted largely by what they see as a threat to their community or, possibly, to their own political self-interest. In the final analysis the commissions, by weighing the relatively few submissions and interventions from the public hearing stage of the process, fulfill their primary responsibility as independent arbiters of competing versions of representational fairness.

Toward More Equitable Districts?

In Canada's four-decade experience with independent electoral boundary commissions, there has been a measurable improvement in the degree to which seats in Parliament and provincial legislatures have become more similar in their populations. This means that there are now fewer differences in the "value" of the votes of Canadians than when elected politicians controlled redistributions.

Figure 3.1 diagrams that fact by comparing the results of redistributions for Commons seats over the past 100 years. A standard of

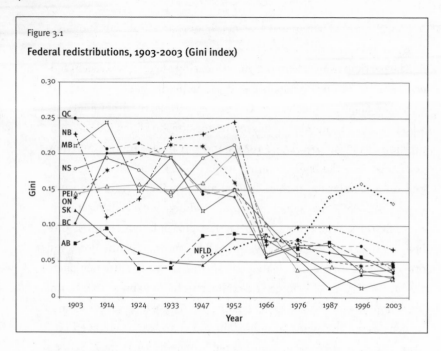

Figure 3.1

Federal redistributions, 1903-2003 (Gini index)

measurement known as the **Gini index** shows that the two provinces in which constituencies were characteristically the most equal before the 1964 legislation, Alberta and Saskatchewan, have remained about the same or slightly closer to equality in riding populations. All other provinces except Newfoundland and Labrador have seen a dramatic improvement in seat equality since the introduction in 1964 of the Electoral Boundaries Readjustment Act. The Newfoundland experience since 1987 reflects the province's small number of federal seats and its commissions' generous use of the statute's "extraordinary circumstances" provision. That provision has enabled the commissioners to construct seats with populations outside the ±25 percent level. In the seven remaining provinces the equality of the vote has increased sharply. In other words, the great majority of Canadians live in ridings in which their vote is on more of a par with their fellow citizens in their province than was ever the case prior to the introduction of independent boundary commissions.

That said, however, it should be remembered that the growing *intra*provincial population equality stands in contrast to the growing *inter*provincial differences in population size. This paradox can be explained by the federalized nature of the process of allocating seats in the Commons combined with the established practice of commissions aiming for a large measure of population equality within each province. As we have seen, the formula for assigning seat numbers to provinces and territories is both constitutionally and statutorily determined. With continued uneven population growth among the provinces, interprovincial variations in district size will remain unavoidable under the current method of allocating Commons seats.

Conclusion

Independent electoral boundary commissions stand as one of the democratic advances of the last half-century in Canadian political institutions. Commissions are widely seen as fair, nonpartisan, and independent bodies assigned a task that previously was performed in a partisan manner by elected politicians. Commissions have sought explicitly to take into account such important and well-understood values as community interests and particular local considerations. They often cannot satisfy all local demands for constructing a district with one set of boundaries rather than another, but given the variety of representational interests they must adjudicate it would be surprising if they could. As well, the process has contributed to democratic electoral practices in Canada by enabling local citizens to express their preferences, to have them weighed in the balance, and to be granted a fair hearing by disinterested decision makers in a way that was never possible before.

But the electoral boundary readjustment process is not without its problems and its critics. The biggest redistribution issue at the federal level has nothing to do with the work of the commissions. Rather it stems from the formula for determining provincial entitlements in the House of Commons. The growing disparity in provincial populations, resting as it does on the application of the grandfather and senatorial clauses every ten years, may prompt the media and disgruntled voters in the faster-growing provinces to call for a new method of determining provincial and territorial entitlements to Commons seats.

As we have seen, the 2001 census showed a demographic trend continued from the previous two or three decades: growth in Ontario, Alberta, and British Columbia outpaced that of the rest of the county. It is difficult to foresee any reapportionment of Commons' seats among the provinces in the next decade that will not provoke public and political controversy about the fairness of the current redistribution formula. What, if anything, can or should be done about the fact that on a per capita basis Prince Edward Islanders have about three-and-a-half times the number of MPs as Ontarians, or that for this decade Saskatchewan will have on average 55,000 fewer voters per federal riding than neighbouring Alberta? Answering these inherently difficult questions of representational fairness will test the ingenuity of lawmakers, and possibly the courts. If the recent population trend continues, the question of the "value" of one person's vote relative to another will continue to plague the periodic representational exercise in the years ahead.

Two hurdles stand in the way of changing the formula: the senatorial and grandfather clauses. The first could be altered only with unanimous approval of Parliament and all provincial legislatures, the second by an amendment to the 1985 federal act. Changing either or both protections is far from an assured thing. Weighed against any pressure to change the current formula will be the benefits that accrue to the smaller provinces and Quebec from an inflated Commons representation. Indeed, a powerful argument against the position taken by those who call for a more equitable population-based allocation of Commons' seats among the provinces can be made on the grounds of Canadian federalism.

Part of the Confederation agreement was that seats in the Commons would be allocated to *provinces*, not to *people*, a principle that remains in the Constitution to this day. This is particularly relevant to any consideration of changing the current formula. Given the absence of a credible and politically salient upper house in Canada, which, as in Australia and the United States, could be fully expected to play a major role in representing provincial interests, the cabinet serves as the critical representational and policy-making unit at the federal level. To enhance their chances of having at least one member of the federal cabinet, the Atlantic provinces, Manitoba, and Saskatchewan can be counted on to oppose any serious attempt to reduce their seat allotments (and, therefore, their presence at the federal cabinet table) in the Commons.

The same can be expected of Quebec, which also benefits from the current floors guaranteeing parliamentary representation. Quebec's gradual demographic decline (the province is now below 25 percent of Canada's total population) has been attenuated in Parliament by the representational floors. Quebec's present level of seventy-five Commons seats (seven more seats than its population warrants) might, of course, be partially reduced by Parliament alone in the years ahead, but the political pressures against doing so can be expected to remain strong. The rules no longer use Quebec as the base for establishing the Commons' size and the entitlement of the other provinces (as they did from 1867 to 1946 and 1974 to 1985), but the province nonetheless retains a pivotal role in determining that entitlement because of the potentially negative political consequences for any federal governing party choosing to alter the formula. Any reduction would be criticized in Quebec as an attack by Ottawa on the province and as a way of trying to diminishing the province's role in the Commons and the cabinet.

Short of unanimous federal and provincial agreement to remove the senatorial floor from the Constitution (a highly unlikely development), the only possible way for Parliament to address the issue is through the grandfather clause. The Lortie Commission had this in mind when it recommended doing away with grandfathered seats on a gradual basis, ensuring that no province would lose more than one seat per decade. This is a sensible compromise between continued adherence to the current formula and the complete elimination of the grandfather guarantee at one fell swoop. With time, the Lortie proposal would help in reducing the interprovincial spread in average Commons' district size.

The issue of citizen participation in federal redistributions remains problematic. The introduction of independent boundary commissions created an opportunity for citizen involvement in the political process. In theory, at least, public hearings provide the means whereby citizens can express their views about the size and shape of an electoral building block. That building block, in turn, captures territorially bounded interests and ultimately plays a critical part in the aggregation of votes and in the conversion of votes into seats in the assemblies. But the hope of widespread public participation has so far not become a reality. Few Canadians have availed themselves of the opportunity to contribute to a commission's deliberations. This is not so much a reflection on the procedure itself (for commission hearings in various parts of a province are widely advertised and commented upon in the media) as it is on the general lack of interest in a subject. Only when local interests are seen as in some way threatened by a commission's plans do the local political elites become sufficiently mobilized to make their views known.

New technologies may open the door to increased public participation. The technology is now available for constructing on a moment's notice a great variety of territorially defined electoral districts of alternative shapes, sizes, and demographic compositions. Elections Canada has invested heavily in developing a computer-based geographic information system that allows redistribution commissioners and members of the public appearing at commission hearings to propose alternative districts based on comprehensive, real-time demographic data. As the technologies and the expertise needed to employ them become more widely available, alternative maps could be more closely scrutinized by commissioners and members of the public. This, in turn, has the potential to enhance the democratic nature of the exercise by increasing public interest in electoral districting.

The real success story of the electoral boundary revolution lies in the fact that independent electoral boundary commissions at both the federal and provincial levels were instituted in the first place. Many parliamentarians and provincial legislators remain uneasy with the changed process, as was demonstrated by Parliament's two legislated delays in beginning the federal redistribution of the 1990s. But however discontented they may be with the results of the current method of drawing constituency boundaries, parliamentarians would be the first to acknowledge that returning to the earlier system is not a realistic option. Partisan gerrymandering as it was once practised in Canada has been relegated to history, and the credibility of political representation in Canada's elected assemblies has been enhanced by the change.

CHAPTER 3

✦ Nonpartisan commissions now determine electoral district boundaries.

✦ The community of interest principle helps to incorporate social, regional, and ethnic considerations in the construction of electoral districts.

✦ "Effective representation" is an ambiguous term open to differing interpretations.

REGISTERING VOTERS

4

Part of the task of any democratic audit is to assess the appropriateness of political and governmental institutions to a society's culture and social values. The purpose of this chapter is to carry out such an assessment of an essential element in the conduct of elections: the method of registering voters, a seemingly prosaic task whose success is profoundly affected by the particular institutional framework within which it is carried out. The methods of registering voters vary from one country or jurisdiction to another, but the basic premise remains the same. No election can be held (certainly no democratic one) without first compiling lists of those who are eligible to vote.

As with the franchise and electoral districting, the voter registration system used by a jurisdiction reveals something about its political culture and social values. Some states are wedded to the idea that individuals eligible to vote are themselves responsible for ensuring that their names are on the voters list. Others see the state as bearing the primary responsibility for compiling lists of electors. Because voter registration may be handled in various ways, the central focus of any assessment should always be on how well one system serves the electorate as opposed to another. How easy is it for voters to become registered, and how complete and accurate are the lists of voters that are used in the election? Those questions involve the accessibility, responsiveness, and inclusiveness of various methods of voter registration.

Compiling the List

Voter registration is at the very heart of our democratic process. Without it, citizens could not legitimately cast the ballot to which they are entitled under section 3 of the Charter. A registration system appropriate to a free and democratic society must be based on three principles: as many qualified citizens should be included on the list as possible; electoral abuse and fraud by voters, parties, and governments must be prevented; and citizens, parties, and candidates must accept the list as an authoritative and definitive catalogue of the electorate. In other words, the registration system must ensure accessibility to all eligible electors, safeguard the interests of the individual and the public, and be widely accepted as a fair, reasonable, and inclusive electoral roll.

On the face of it, compiling a voters list seems a straightforward, uncomplicated business. It amounts to including the name and address of every eligible voter on a final tally of electors so that on election day voters will be confident that they will be listed among those entitled to cast a vote at their local polling district. The theory is simple, the reality more complicated.

A number of social, demographic, and political variables intersect to make the construction of a voters list more difficult than it might at first seem. No matter how it is performed, the task is complicated by population mobility, human error and oversight, information-gathering problems, and technological glitches. No country has yet designed the ideal voter registration system in the sense of ensuring that its list is a complete and accurate one. It is fair to predict that none ever will.

At various stages of our history, Canada has tried different methods of preparing its voter registration lists. Before the current electronically based "permanent" electoral list, the most common method over the decades, and the one with which Canadians still have had most experience, was door-to-door enumeration. But these have by no means been the only models. For the first fifty years after Confederation, federal and provincial voters lists were manipulated in a blatantly partisan fashion by the various governments. Because the franchise in the early post-Confederation years was tied to property ownership, the lists of eligible electors were typically drawn from local assessment rolls. From 1867 to 1885 there were no federal lists per se. Instead, to vote in a federal election a male property-owner had to be on a provincial list, which, in turn, was almost certainly drawn from local assessment lists.

Revisions and corrections were made at the local level as well. In Ontario changes were made by county court judges, whereas in Quebec, New Brunswick, and Nova Scotia the task was handled by various municipal officials. It made little difference how revisions were made, for whether an elector's name appeared on the list was at least as much a matter of partisanship as legal entitlement. The names on the electoral lists resulted largely from the political circumstances in a riding, the party in control of the local election machinery, the known political allegiance of the individual voter, and possibly, the partisan leanings of the appeal officials or judges.

In tandem with the changes to the federal franchise laws, the construction of lists of voters oscillated between the two levels of government. Federal voting rolls were based on provincial ones between 1867 and 1885, 1898 and 1917, and 1920 and 1929. In the intervals, federal lists were compiled, sometimes on the basis of door-to-door enumerations but more frequently on the basis of a set of pre-existing federal election lists with annual revisions. Not until 1938 did Parliament approve legislation calling for a national door-to-door enumeration at the time of each federal election. Soon all the provinces followed suit with election-driven enumeration for their own provincial elections.

To Norman Ward, Canadian history to 1938 demonstrated that "any scheme of 'standing' lists, which are kept up-to-date by regular revisions, apparently cannot work in a country which has heavy internal movements of population." Moreover, according to Ward, any system that "puts the onus on individuals and organizations [to ensure names are on the lists] is sure to produce inaccurate and unsatisfactory lists, for the circumstances governing the actual compilation of the lists will inevitably tend to be irrelevant to the lists' purpose" (Ward 1950, 204). These comments are worth remembering as we make our way through our analysis of Canada's voter registration system.

Who's Responsible: Governments or Individuals?

Voter registration systems around the world are of two different kinds, according to where the responsibility for initiating the registration lies: with the individual or with the government. The United States, for example, leaves it up to individual citizens to ensure that they are on the list. But its system is far from perfect. Although enormous voter registration drives are held throughout the United States in advance of every election, and even though Congress approved a "Motor Voter" program in 1993 whereby those obtaining or renewing drivers licences would have the relevant information added to their state's voters list, the lists of potential voters are far from complete. At the time of the 2000 presidential election, it is estimated that only 78 percent of eligible American citizens were registered. The group with the smallest share of its potential electorate registered was the young. Only 59 percent of Americans eighteen to twenty-four years of age were on the voters list (Wolfinger, Highton, and Mullin 2002, 16). These low figures, which are without parallel in advanced liberal democracies, call into question the appropriateness of leaving registration up to the individual.

Voter registration in Canada has always rested on a different premise. Wherever door-to-door enumerations were held at the onset of an election campaign, the government played the key role in the preparation of voters lists. With the exception of British Columbia, the provinces have traditionally relied on government-sponsored enumerations. More recently, Parliament approved the establishment of an electronic database known as the National Register of Electors. This regularly updated and revised collection of elector information managed by Elections Canada derives its data from a number of sources: individual electors, federal departments and agencies, and some provincial government data files.

Of the provinces, British Columbia has a long history of a voter registration system unique in Canada. With the exception of the period of the Second World War, since the nineteenth century British Columbia has used either a revised voters list compiled at the previous election or, more recently, a continuously updated voters register. The current register is maintained on an ongoing basis with voter information from the previous election; new voter registrations via either online forms or Election BC's 1-800 telephone number; data files provided by the province's Insurance Corporation and Vital Statistics branch; and updates generated by municipalities that use the provincial register for local elections. These sources of information are further supplemented by a province-wide enumeration carried out three years after every election. For the first time in 1999 this enumeration was conducted first by post and then, for those residences from which no reply had been received, door-to-door surveys. Thus the British Columbia register relies on both government and the individual for its construction and maintenance.

Little changed in the federal registration system between 1938 and 1997. Two enumerators were appointed for every urban polling division in a constituency, and one in every rural one. Appointed by a constituency's returning officer, the enumerators were selected from lists supplied by the two candidates receiving the highest number of votes in the preceding election. This bipartisan element of the process was intended to serve as a check against possible registration fraud. Because enumerators were paid on a per voter basis there was a built-in incentive to try to ensure as complete and accurate a list of voters as possible. The more names of qualified voters that the enumerators were able to include the greater their financial compensation. Door-to-door enumeration is premised on the idea that the state can play a role in making the electoral registration process widely inclusive of the citizenry. That is missing in the American system where the onus for getting on an electoral roll rests with the individual.

Canada's door-to-door enumeration recognized as well the importance of volunteerism to the well-being of political parties at the local level. A healthy democratic system rests on a number of practices and institutions. Of these, parties in the constituencies are among the most important. In R.K. Carty's term, local parties are fighting in "the trenches" of Canadian politics, which is to say the local political fronts that are vitally critical to the success of a party, its leader, and its candidates (Carty 1988). By drawing enumerators from the ranks of the women and men who serve as local party volunteers during an election campaign, Canada recognized the importance of human capital in the political process.

By definition, party volunteers at the constituency level are often multitaskers. They stuff envelopes, operate phone banks, solicit funds, campaign and deliver party literature on a door-to-door basis, scrutineer on election day, and manage constituency offices. They are, in a very real sense, the backbone of the local party. Rarely are they paid by the party or the candidate for their work. With them a candidate is not guaranteed electoral victory, but without them no candidate can win. (The importance of party volunteers is considered more fully in another book in the Democratic Audit series, Cross 2004.) Appointing many of these individuals as enumerators recognized the fact that the health of Canadian electoral democracy depended on their contribution to parties as civic-minded volunteers. The state was willing to acknowledge that contribution by offering them a small financial reward for taking part in a critically important exercise.

Between 1938 and 1997 the preparation of the preliminary list of electors (which was the product of the door-to door canvass carried out over several days by the enumerators) was followed by a number of days of revisions. The revising period enabled qualified electors who had been left off the earlier list, or those for whom incorrect information had been given, to have changes made by a local revising officer. Over a number of federal elections using enumeration and revision, Elections Canada found that the lists captured between 95 and 97.5 percent of Canada's eligible electorate (Courtney and Smith 1991, 365 and 451; Elections Canada 2001c, 67). In 1988, for example, the number of qualified electors not included in the final tally averaged roughly three thousand for each of the 295 ridings in the country or about eight for each of the 53,000 polling districts. Compared to other countries that rely on government to play the dominant role in constructing the registry of electors, these are impressive figures. It is difficult to imagine a method of registering voters that could have been more inclusive and up-to-date than the system Canada had in place for nearly two-thirds of the twentieth century.

Time for a Change?

Door-to-door enumeration as Canadians had known it for sixty years was not to last. In the period between 1957 and 1988 cracks had begun to appear in the process, leading Elections Canada to recommend a massive overhaul in how voter registration would take place for federal elections. The problems leading to the change in voter registration systems are outlined below. In general, they were the result of three developments. First, the country experienced a record number of federal elections – twelve – over a thirty-year period. On two occasions (1957-8 and 1979-80) two elections were held within less than ten months of one another. Second, the electorate doubled between 1957 to 1988, going from 8.9 million to 17.6 million registered voters. This was in part a result of lowering the voting age from twenty-one to eighteen and in part because of natural growth and immigration following the Second World War. Third, urban Canada's growth vastly outpaced that of rural Canada. Not only that, but the major urban centres developed into ethnically, linguistically, and culturally mixed societies.

Together, these demographic and political developments were alleged to have placed the traditional and familiar process of enumeration under stress. It had been designed in a period of Canadian history when elections were less frequent and when voters were fewer in number and less concentrated in urban and metropolitan areas. Although in general terms the system had adapted well to postwar changes, nonetheless several problems specific to enumerations were flagged by Elections Canada and accepted by the Chrétien government as sufficient reason for fundamentally changing the method of voter registration.

From the early 1970s on, a number of returning officers reported difficulty in finding, training, and retaining enumerators. This paralleled the experience of political parties at the riding level, which had increasing trouble drawing volunteers (especially young recruits) into their local campaign operations at election time. By the late 1980s and early 1990s, local parties and constituency returning officers were only two of countless organizations and structures traditionally dependent on volunteers to experience problems of recruitment. This phenomenon was characterized by Robert Putnam in the United States in his book Bowling Alone, a study documenting the decline of social networks and citizen engagement (Putnam 2000). The experience of many traditional volunteer organizations in Canada that had long served as pillars of our civic society (such as service clubs, charitable organizations, and church groups) was similar to that described by Putnam in America.

The relatively low pay scale did nothing to assist the search for enumerators (who earned, on average, roughly $300 for intermittent work that lasted several days). Nor did the fact that enumerators were required, by law, to canvass every residence in their polling district. For some urban enumerators this was said to be an unattractive option, particularly in the evening (often the only time potential voters would be home) in areas where the enumerators' security might be at risk. The increasingly mixed linguistic composition of Canada's major cities was claimed as well to be a hindrance, for enumerators in some polls found they were unable to speak to potential voters in their native language.

Although published reports of problems with the enumeration system overstated the magnitude of the difficulties that voters, enumerators, and returning officers faced at election time, the perception was created of widespread failure of the system. Calls for "something better" in the way of voter registration came from the press in some metropolitan centres and from a handful of dissatisfied MPs. The central issues in the controversy (principally the short-term employment of sufficient numbers of qualified enumerators and the assurance that complete door-to-door canvasses would be carried out) prompted Elections Canada to advance a plan for a fundamental overhaul of the registration system. (For a fuller account of enumeration problems encountered federally and in one of the provinces, and of possible solutions that could have maintained the traditional voter enumeration process at the federal level, see Courtney and Smith 1991, 358-72, and Elections BC 1999.)

The National Register of Electors

The shortage of enumerators and the problems with the enumeration process were not the only, nor indeed the principal, factors leading to a fundamental recrafting of the voter registration system. The government, and ultimately Parliament, were convinced by a twofold promise of better things to come. The argument was made that replacing door-to-door enumeration with a <u>continuously maintained electoral register would permit shorter election campaigns</u>. As well, it was claimed that a so-called permanent register of voters would save the taxpayers substantial amounts of money. Both were eminently attractive reasons to the elected politicians who ultimately decided the fate of the traditional enumeration process. Before examining those reasons a brief outline of the new Register is in order.

The Register itself has been designed to operate as a centralized and regularly updated record of the Canadian electorate. Its information comes from a variety of sources. Like British Columbia's voter registration system, the federal Register relies on both government and individuals to ensure a substantial measure of completeness and accuracy. Since being established in 1997 from the lists produced in the enumeration for that year's federal election, the Register has served as a database of qualified Canadian electors. It contains each person's name, address, sex, and date of birth. Canadians may choose not to be listed in the Register, but in order to vote an unlisted individual needs to have his or her name added to the list during the revision period, at an advance poll, or at the poll on election day.

Information to keep the Register up-to-date is received regularly by Elections Canada from a variety of sources. For example, new Canadian citizens can be added to the Register by indicating on a consent box on their citizenship application form that they wish Citizenship and Immigration Canada to forward that information to Elections Canada. (Unlike Australia, Canada does not *require* newly eligible voters, such as eighteen-year-olds or new citizens, to register). Elections Canada also has an agreement with the Canada Customs and Revenue Agency to supply information pertinent to the register of electors. Those filing an income tax return can give consent on their form to allow CCRA to transfer the necessary demographic information to Elections Canada, an option some 83 to 84 percent of Canadian tax filers have exercised.

As well, information is drawn from various provincial departments and agencies to augment or to check against existing entries on the list. These include motor vehicle licensing authorities; electoral agencies with permanent lists, such as British Columbia's and now Quebec's; and vital statistics registrars. In return, information from the National Register of Electors is available for sharing with provincial or territorial bodies responsible for establishing lists of electors. These include provincial, territorial, and municipal jurisdictions as well as school boards.

To keep the Register as current as possible in the event an election is called unexpectedly and the preliminary lists need to be transferred from Ottawa to the more than three hundred returning officers, something akin to voter revision is more or less continually under way in the Register's central office in Ottawa. This is necessitated by the fact that the Register deals with a highly mobile and changing population. Roughly 20 percent of Canadians move every year. Some of these, such as university students, move two or three times in the course of a twelve-month period. Whether a move is across the street or across the country makes no difference to the Register, for both constitute a change of address and, possibly, of constituency. In addition, each year close to 400,000 Canadians turn eighteen, 200,000 become citizens, and another 200,000 die. These additions or deletions too must be entered into the Register. To be useful on a moment's notice at the beginning of an election period, the Register is entirely dependent on the quality and completeness of its database.

Register Rationale

SHORTER CAMPAIGNS

The length of federal campaigns has long been a source of contention for politicians, who have to endure day after day of campaigning, rallies, strategy meetings, media interviews, canvassing, speechmaking, debates, and so on. In addition to their own constituency obligations, party leaders, cabinet ministers, and other prominent candidates in all parties spend a great deal of their time criss-crossing the country. More often than not they put in exceedingly long days. Modern political campaigning can be an exhausting activity with election day seemingly always too far away. Understandably, shorter campaigns sound attractive to those who bear the brunt of a campaign.

A decade or so before Parliament was persuaded of the merits of adopting the National Register of Electors, a first step was taken to reduce the number of days of an election campaign. Through amendments to the Canada Elections Act campaigns were shortened by 17 percent, from sixty days to fifty. A further reduction would have been agreed to had it not been for one stumbling block – the door-to-door enumeration system. Enumeration (which began after the issuance of election writs) was faulted by its critics for taking too long and for unnecessarily lengthening the period between an election writ being issued and an election being held. Without the time needed to hire and train enumerators and compile polling district lists, critics of enumeration estimated that at least ten days could be lopped off a federal campaign.

The assertion that "less is more" when it comes to election campaigns is worth examining. Some specialists in comparative politics note that British and Australian elections run for four to five weeks at the most and that Canada could easily do the same. Although all three share a parliamentary form of government, however, Canadian politics has a level of complexity missing from the other two countries. Considerable social, linguistic, political, geographic, and regional differences exist between those countries (particularly Britain) and

Canada. For example, Canadian federal elections are held irregularly (at least once every five years but more often if the prime minister decides) in a campaign for control of a *single* parliamentary chamber. Although Australia shares with Canada a federal system of government, its parliamentary elections must come at least every three years and they are for *two* chambers – all of the lower house and (at least) one-half of the upper house. More frequent elections for two houses of parliament provide Australia with the rationale for holding shorter rather than longer campaigns.

Parliamentary elections in Britain are conducted over a geographic area that is tiny by comparison with Canada. It is so small, in fact, that major party leaders normally return to London each evening after campaigning in the country. That enables them to meet every morning with reporters from the major print and broadcast media, all of which are located in London. A similar practice is simply out of the question in Canada where distances are far greater, the media are less concentrated, and the country's regional and social diversity entails certain campaign rituals. To cite one example, Canada's bilingual character affects election campaign length in this country. Leaders' debates are in both official languages and therefore twice as frequent as in Britain and Australia. This has the practical effect of doubling the time spent by the leaders and their handlers in debates and in preparation for them.

Canadian politicians were not alone in wanting campaigns to end sooner rather than later. The media often reflected that sentiment, and so did those voters who said they "tired" of a campaign well before it ended. Curiously, however, the evidence that the public preferred shorter election campaigns is inconclusive. On the one hand, many of the 120 briefs presented to the Lortie Commission during its public hearings supported their criticisms of enumeration by citing the need for shorter election campaigns. Yet on the other hand, in a list of problems and shortcomings of Canada's enumeration system, the items analyzed over a nearly twenty-year period in Elections Canada's publications demonstrated the opposite. The length of the election campaign was not seen by the voting public as an issue requiring reform.

Instead the public's major concerns were consistently the quality of enumeration and the possible exclusion of eligible voters from lists if their quality flagged (Courtney and Smith 1991, 370-1).

As with the "right" size for an elected assembly, the "proper" length of election campaigns is impossible to determine categorically. What is right for one jurisdiction may be wrong for another, and what is right for one election may be wrong for another. The critical democratic test is whether the citizenry has sufficient time to contemplate the alternative parties and leaders competing for office and to digest from the media accounts the differences in policies and personalities among the alternative teams of office seekers. With the adoption in 1996 of a plan whereby a National Register of Electors could be constructed and maintained on an ongoing basis, Parliament succeeded, as the politicians had hoped, in reducing the length of campaigns. They were cut from a minimum election period of forty-seven days to thirty-six, which amounted to a 23 percent reduction. Federal campaigns are now 40 percent shorter than they were two decades ago. Once we have conducted three or four elections under the new, shorter campaigns (1999 was the first), election observers will have to assess whether thirty-six days provide sufficient time for full media and voter appraisal of parties, leaders, candidates, and policies, and whether shorter campaigns work to the advantage of incumbents and to the disadvantage of challengers.

In many cases, as Canada's national election studies have confirmed, voter attitudes remain largely unchanged at the close of a campaign from what they had been at the outset. That would suggest, reductio ad absurdum, that one-day election campaigns would save us all (voters, candidates, leaders, and parties) time, effort, and money. Clearly that is not an option in any democratic system. But thirty-six as opposed to, say, forty-seven days? Kim Campbell and the Progressive Conservatives would have welcomed such an abbreviated campaign in 1993. Eleven days before the election there was a spread of fifteen percentage points between the Tories and the Liberals (22 percent and 37 percent respectively) and the Conservatives led Reform by four percentage points (22 percent to 18 percent). By the end of the campaign, Campbell's Conservatives had fallen behind the Liberals by twenty-five percentage points and Reform by three. Only two Tory MPs were elected after forty-seven days of campaigning, without doubt considerably fewer than had the election been held on the thirty-sixth day. However infrequent such cases may be, the 1993 federal election demonstrates that campaign length can make a substantial difference to the fate of individual parties and to the outcome of an election. (Election polling data over the period of the 1993 campaign are from Frizzell and Westell 1994, 101-2.)

COST SAVINGS

Members of Parliament were also persuaded in 1996 by Elections Canada's promise of future cost savings if the National Register of Electors were adopted. Not having to hire 100,000 enumerators for up to ten days during an election period was seen as a major factor in lower projected voter registration costs in the future. The start-up costs (for computers, data exchange software, recruiting and training of new permanent staff, and the like) attributed to the new Register were estimated by Elections Canada at $41 million. These would be more than offset by projected savings of $138 million over a series of six federal elections. Such figures were music to the ears of a government engaged at that very time in substantial budget paring. During the parliamentary debate stage, MPs made much of the attractiveness of a regularly updated Register as a cheaper and more fiscally prudent method of compiling the voters lists.

So far, the predicted savings have materialized. After one federal election using the Register (2000), Elections Canada is optimistic that its savings projections are accurate and may even be exceeded in the course of the next few elections. According to Elections Canada the initial capital investment in the Register and its corresponding maintenance costs were substantially less than anticipated. The initial outlay might therefore be recovered after one election rather than, as projected, two. That saving, in turn, has enabled Elections Canada to project continued "costs avoided" in the years ahead at a faster pace than the agency had originally anticipated (Elections Canada 2001b; 2002).

As encouraging as the early signs may be, a word of caution is in order. How cost effective the new method of voter registration will prove to be in the long run remains to be seen. Only after several elections can the question of savings be truly addressed. When it comes, that exercise will, at one level, amount to a relatively simple examination of such trade-offs as the financial gains made from moving from 100,000 enumerators and a forty-seven-day election campaign to a continuously maintained list that is less labour intensive and a thirty-six-day election period. At another level, however, the exercise will be decidedly more complex.

The complexities stem from the variety of special initiatives that must be undertaken under the new registration system that were not needed under the old one. These include writing letters to close to 400,000 young people each year who, upon turning 18, are urged by Elections Canada to get their names on the Register. It also includes "targeted revisions" of special groups or areas, which are strikingly similar to the former door-to-door enumerations. Carried out by several thousand revising agents in the second and third week of a campaign, targeted revisions are aimed at ensuring that approximately a million voters (the figure established in the 2000 election) in areas of high mobility and of new residential development are on the Register. The costs of establishing and maintaining agreements with other governments and agencies for the transfer and use of their data files will also have be factored into any cost-benefit analysis of the Register.

Finally, there are, of course, the costs of continually maintaining and updating the list. Under enumeration/revision, lists of electors were prepared when they were needed, which is to say when an election or a by-election was called. These were relatively rare occurrences, typically every three or four years for a general election. The lists were not maintained between elections, and thus no costs were incurred, because a new set of lists would be designed once another election was called. The lists produced by enumeration and revision were not perfect, as we have seen, but because they were drawn up shortly before election day they had the great advantage of being current and complete to the level of between 95 and 97.5 percent of eligible voters.

The National Register of Electors, on the other hand, is maintained from one day to the next and from one year to the next without any occasion at the federal level on which to be put into use. Is it cost-effective to incur expenditures to maintain a list (a list that, as we will see, still has to undergo large-scale modifications in the course of an election campaign) when it is not needed? Only time and several elections will definitively answer that question. (For comparative costs of maintaining British Columbia's voter register and door-to-door enumerations in other provinces and at the federal level in the late 1980s, see Courtney and Smith 1991, 381-3).

Reality Check

All in all, the new voter registration system had many highly saleable features. Election campaigns would become shorter, taxpayers would benefit, and information would be shared by federal and provincial electoral authorities. In a country more often noted for its jurisdictional rivalries than cooperation, the last was a significant achievement. But the Register of Electors did not get off to a faultless start. The only experience to date at the federal level with the Register (the 2000 election) shows there is room for improvement. Without it, voter participation and citizen inclusiveness in the electoral process could be adversely affected in the long run.

Practically speaking, how complete and accurate is the list? Elections Canada estimated that the final count at the time of the 2000 election showed that 95 percent of the total eligible electorate ended up on the lists, although one scholar claims that 93 percent is a more accurate figure (Black 2002; Elections Canada 2001c, 103). Neither figure represents an increase over the previous system in the share of eligible citizens included in the final list of registered voters.

Moreover, the total figures disguise the number of transactions needed to produce an electoral Register of that level of completeness. This can be seen by comparing the number of changes made to the respective systems in the final weeks or days of the 1997 enumerated election and the 2000 Register election. The lists of electors produced in the early stages of the campaign on a riding-by-riding basis for the enumeration in 1997 gave the count of electors at 19,663,478. Of that number 229,000 were described in the final tally as having been duplicate entries of voters' names and a further 9,000 were found to be deceased between the time of enumeration and election day. These eliminated entries amounted to 1.2 percent of the initial lists, leaving the number of registered voters for that election at 19,425,478.

By contrast, in the 2000 election the new Register, which had been constructed initially from the enumerated lists prepared for the 1997 election and then continually updated over the intervening three and one-half years from various federal and provincial sources, produced a far less accurate reading of the electorate. The lists showed 21,243,473 registered electors at the outset of the 2000 election campaign. But of that number 614,000 were later found to have been duplicate entries and a further 177,000 deceased. The final registered electorate came to 20,452,473. Together the duplicate and deceased entries amounted to 3.7 percent of the initial lists, or three times what they had been under door-to-door enumeration barely three years earlier.

Revision is an essential part of any voter registration system. This proved to be even more the case with the Register in 2000 than ever before. By the time the polls closed on the 2000 election the 301 ridings had collectively handled more than 3.6 million revisions to the lists presented to them by Elections Canada only thirty-six days before. This was nearly three times the 1.3 million revisions made in 1997. The 2000 total was made up of 2.8 million additions and address changes, 400,000 removals, and 400,000 other corrections. Each of these required at least one bookkeeping entry into the Register.

The alterations to the list were composed of electors who registered during targeted revisions in, for example, door-to-door enumerations of such areas as new suburbs and university and college campuses; electors who registered in response to special initiatives undertaken by Elections Canada or during the advance polling period; and electors who registered at their polling station on election day. At 1.05 million, election-day registrants constituted by far the largest single group of additions or changes to the list. This number vastly exceeded the 660,000 election-day registrants that Elections Canada had predicted (Elections Canada 1997, 15; 2001c, 74).

Newspaper reports, radio talk shows, university classroom discussions, and coffee row chatter all pointed in the same direction in 2000. There was a degree of confusion about the registration process that was without parallel in recent electoral history. This was especially true of young and highly mobile Canadians. Elections Canada's print and television advertisements warning Canadians "You can't vote if you're not on the list" did not help. The statement was technically true. In order to vote, all qualified electors either had to be included among those registered on a polling district's preliminary list or be added to the list through revision or on election day. Nonetheless the advertisement's wording confused the public's understanding of the new system. This could be easily remedied in the future by Elections Canada presenting a simple, positive message: "You can be added to the list when you go to vote."

Electors were not the only Canadians who were at a loss in 2000. Elections Canada reported following the election that a majority of candidates and political party representatives "indicated a low degree of satisfaction with the preliminary lists of electors." For their part returning officers "reported having to deal with widespread or major complaints about the preliminary lists of electors, indicating that the accuracy of the lists did not meet their expectations." In an Elections Canada survey, candidates, political parties, returning officers, and academics all agreed that greater information needed to be provided in future to the public about voter registration procedures and that the accuracy of the lists of electors needed to be improved (Elections Canada 2000b, 7-8).

In truth, the great majority of Canada's electors knew that they were included on the preliminary list and that they were properly informed of that. The 2000 Canadian Election Study found that 83 percent of its postelection sample (n = 2,898) had received information cards showing that their names were on the first list. But what of the 17 percent (an unprecedented number by the standards of earlier enumerations) who were either not informed or improperly informed of their voter registration? Those who were most likely either to have been omitted from the Register or to experience difficulties getting on the list tended overwhelmingly to be the young, poor, mobile, tenants, and those with limited language skills (White 2002, 4).

Of those who had not received a card, 48 percent had tried to get their name on the list and 51 percent had not. Of those who did try, 60 percent said it was easy or quite easy to get on the list, whereas 40 percent found it difficult or very difficult. Four percent said they were never able to get on the list (Blais et al. 2002, 60, and information provided by the Canadian Election Study investigators). Homeless citizens were treated no differently by the new system than the old, but 24 percent of all Aboriginal people and 26 percent of Canada's young voters (aged eighteen to twenty-five) did not receive voter information cards confirming their entries on the preliminary lists of electors (according to an Ipsos-Reid survey cited in Elections Canada 2000b, 7).

The move to the Register has replaced a system in which the responsibility for generating the voters lists lay almost entirely with the state with one in which a larger number of Canadian citizens (17 percent in 2000) must now take the initiative to ensure that their names are on the list. That this treats potential voters differentially is clear from some of the evaluations made to date of the Register. According to one political scientist, those most likely to have been left off the Register of Electors are "precisely those groups that are most in need of assistance from the state in exercising their democratic rights" (White 2002, 4). To another student of the subject, so-called permanent voters lists contribute to "increasing participation inequality" because, unlike door-to-door enumeration, the Register requires of individuals proactive "procedures that make it more diffi-cult for the less well-off to participate" (Black 2000, 20; see also Black 2003). These observations echo Norman Ward's early prediction about some of the problems inherent in a "permanent" voter register.

What the 2000 federal election suggests is a mixed reception for the Register. Not only did some voters have either no interest or no success in getting on the list, but some demographically defined groups had differential success rates with registration. Inclusion on the voter registry was more likely for older, less mobile Canadians than for younger, mobile, and Aboriginal citizens. The same, of course, was true of door-to-door enumerations: society's most mobile citizens were less likely to have been captured by enumeration than those who moved less frequently. Nonetheless a comparison of the problems associated with voter registration in the 1997 and 2000 elections demonstrates that the registration systems differed in their capacity to include the more mobile and less advantaged citizens and to require markedly fewer last-minute corrections to the voters list.

These concerns prompted Elections Canada to propose some rela-tively minor changes to the legislation governing the National Regis-ter of Electors (Elections Canada 2001a, 13-21). Whether these will improve the accuracy of the new voter registration system at the time of the next federal election remains to be seen. What was not pro-posed, but may be necessary if the Register is to be more current and complete at the time an election is called, is a more major reform – something of a "back to the future" reform. Biennial or triennial door-to-door enumerations may well be needed to supplement the continu-ously maintained electoral roll.

Tried in a number of jurisdictions that operate with some form of permanent electoral roll, including Australia and British Columbia, door-to-door enumerations held at regular intervals between elections have a good deal to commend them. They offer election officials plenty of time to hire and train enumerators and, subsequent to the enumera-tion, to update and correct the existing Register. They offer voters the chance to bring their entry in the Register up to date. Elections held subsequent to a regular revision of the voters list draw on an electoral database that is more current and comprehensive. If such a reform were adopted in Canada the much-vaunted "last" federal door-to-door enumeration held prior to the 1997 election would turn out not to have been the final one after all.

Whatever changes may be in store for the Register, a general observation about a feature of enumeration missing from the new process is nonetheless warranted. We know that voter turnout in the 2000 federal election plunged to an unprecedented low. Barely 61 percent of those on the voters list (composed of the Register at the outset of the election period, revisions during the campaign, and election-day registrants) turned out to vote. A number of reasons for such a record low rate of participation have been offered by students of that election, and it is not the purpose of this work to reiterate them (see Blais et al. 2002, chap. 3). But could it be that there is a link between the absence of a nationwide door-to-door enumeration and the drop in electoral participation?

A system that places the onus for registration on the state rather than on the citizen, and that is coupled with an election-driven, door-to-door enumeration, serves as a personal reminder by the community of the positive value that it places on electoral participation by its citizens. The approach of a pending election is heralded through human contact. That is the judgment of several observers of voter registration systems, including the chief electoral officer of Manitoba, who cited with approval a study by his province's Law Reform Commission on voter registration. That commission found that enumeration produced a largely complete and accurate list of electors at relatively low cost in a short space of time. Its "final bonus" was that it "*induces community participation*, which is important during an election" (Balasko 1990, 23, emphasis added).

To David Smith, enumeration has a social as well as a cultural benefit. Enumeration, in his view, is "distinctive for the human contact that occurs between the potential voter and the compiler of the voters' list." The process offers immense possibilities, for example, in the socialization of new Canadian citizens into the political process. In metropolitan areas long marked by high rates of immigration, enumeration can represent, in Professor Smith's words, "an important admission stage to the electoral process for newly enfranchised citizens" (Smith 1991, 37).

The personal doorstep contact that brings with it, at least implicitly, a message to take part in a forthcoming election is no doubt better suited to encourage new Canadians or tax filers to turn out for the election than a box checked on a citizenship form or a tax return months or years prior to an election. Human contact has the potential to positively reinforce a civic good – that is, taking part in an election. Data banks and information transferred among government agencies do nothing to remind voters of an important civic responsibility. One observes here a possible paradox worth tracking in the years ahead: does a more technology-driven and impersonal enumeration system contribute to lower political participation levels? It is too early in the history of the new process to answer that question definitively, but modernizing voter registration may have come at the cost of a socializing feature of enumeration.

Conclusion

By itself, the franchise is worth little. What is needed to give effect to the right to vote are accessible, user-friendly electoral institutions and election officials whose honesty and integrity are unquestioned. The voter registration system examined in this chapter is yet another part of the institutional apparatus of Canadian elections.

With the gradual extension of the franchise at both the federal and provincial levels throughout the twentieth century, an increasing number of citizens became accustomed to door-to-door enumerations carried out shortly before each election. This system was not without its faults, as we have seen, but it had one attractive feature that, characteristically for a subtle and less tangible cultural benefit, was ignored by MPs during the parliamentary debate on change. Enumeration was an in-person reminder of a forthcoming election and of a citizen's right to vote.

In less than a decade voter registration in Canada has entered the age of modern technology in a major way. Indeed, during the debates in Parliament and the media about the appropriateness of abandoning door-to-door enumeration in favour of a Register, the suitability of computer technology was frequently cited in support of the change. As the following chapter explains, a similar technologically driven argument has been made regarding Internet voting. What is striking about institutional changes that rest on advances in technology is that they often gloss over the socially valid features of the arrangements that are about to be replaced. Such was the fate of door-to-door enumerations. The role that the state played in reminding citizens of an approaching election and of their inclusion among those entitled to vote had a value that is now lost (except in the areas where a targeted revision takes place during the first two weeks of a campaign) in the facelessness of data banks and information transfers among government agencies and departments.

The overhaul of Canada's voter registration system in the mid-1990s was qualitatively different from earlier reforms made to the franchise and electoral redistricting. The franchise was expanded gradually in Canada over the course of many decades until, more than a century after Confederation, it cut a wide and inclusive swathe across the citizenry. This evolution amounted to a process of gradual democratization. Changes to the process of drawing electoral districts were judged to have been long overdue when, in the second half of the twentieth century, they were put into place. For decades prior to the change governing parties had been faulted by their political opponents, the media, academics, and concerned members of the general public for self-interestedly creating ridings of curious shapes and widely varying populations with little more than their own electoral survival in mind. In relinquishing the task of drawing electoral districts to independent commissions, politicians responded to public criticisms and endowed a new institutional procedure with an almost instant legitimacy. Both the enlargement of the franchise and the reforms in the electoral redistribution process signalled a maturing democracy. The evolution of the franchise amounted to an expansionist phase of Canadian democracy and the changes to electoral districting were of a reformist character.

The switch to a National Register of Electors, on the other hand, was neither expansionist, in the sense of adding to the enrolment lists, nor reformist, in the sense of responding to decades-old calls for substantial improvement to a politically opportunistic procedure. The switch was justified not in terms of democratic theory but on entirely pragmatic grounds: operational difficulties with enumeration, the desire for shorter campaigns and cost savings, and the promises held out by new technology. Whether the problems of door-to-door enumeration could have been successfully dealt with is by now a moot point. The dramatic changes made to the method of registering voters less than a decade ago replaced an established, functioning institutional practice that was well-understood by the electorate. The test of the new Register in the years ahead will be to become as established a part of Canadian elections and as well understood by voters as the method it replaced.

Chapter 4

- Door-to-door enumerations prior to Canadian elections have been replaced by a continuously updated list of electors.

- Federal election campaigns are now shorter than ever before.

- To ensure accuracy and currency the Register of Electors may have to be supplemented periodically with door-to-door enumerations.

5

ELECTORAL MACHINERY:
FROM PARTISANSHIP TO PROFESSIONALISM

Judged by today's standards, the conduct of elections in the early post-Confederation period seems extraordinarily loose and arbitrary. Canadians have come to expect our election officials to be nonpartisan. We place a premium on the secrecy of the ballot. We count on the fairest possible administration of elections and counting of ballots. Canadians are accustomed to all voting on the same day, whether the election is federal or provincial, and to hearing the results soon after all polls have been closed. Our expectations today are far from the reality of nineteenth-century elections. In 135 years we have moved from partisanship to a large measure of professionalism in the administration of our elections. This in turn has helped to assure Canadian voters of elections that are open and accessible to those who wish to cast a ballot.

Canada's first elections could scarcely have been more different. We would not consider them democratic in the sense in which that term is now used, although in fairness they were not materially worse than those in nineteenth-century Britain, the United States, and other countries with which we often compare ourselves. As we saw in Chapter 3, inclusiveness, as measured by the number of people eligible to vote, was in the order of 15 to 20 percent for the first three decades after Confederation. The increased responsiveness of governments and public officials to calls for reforms of the electoral machinery resulted in, among other things, the subsequent growth of the electorate. Many of the obvious flaws of Canada's election administration were corrected within a decade of Confederation, but other improvements in the federal, and more particularly the provincial, levels came intermittently over a much longer period of time.

Without doubt the greatest single improvement in the administration of elections in Canada came with the establishment of the offices of our various chief electoral officers. The first of these independent, nonpartisan institutions charged with ensuring a fair and open electoral process was created by the Parliament of Canada in 1920. Provincial governments, sometimes unwillingly, gradually followed suit in response to opposition, media, and public calls for a move away from partisan electoral administration.

In 1867 the machinery by which elections were conducted was firmly in the hands of the politicians, notably the governing party and cabinet. Those chosen to conduct the elections were known partisans who were destined to be replaced by supporters of the other party upon the defeat of their political benefactors. In the words of a distinguished authority on Canada's electoral system, the country's early electoral machinery amounted to "a continual temptation to the unscrupulous to seek party advantage by tinkering with it" (Ward 1950, 153). Liberals and Conservatives alike played by the same rulebook at both levels of government. Electoral administration was seen as a critical institutional mechanism to be manipulated for the good of those in office.

The remarkable transformation in Canada's electoral machinery stands as a major accomplishment in Canada's electoral history. Voters at both levels of government can with reasonable assurance now count on the administration and oversight of elections by nonpartisan officials charged with the fair application of their respective election laws. One measure of the strength of Canada's electoral machinery has, since the 1970s, come from international agencies and emerging democracies, which have regularly called upon Canada to provide impartial election observers or expert assistance in running fair and open elections.

That said, there is room for improvement in Canada. The long delays at the polling stations and the mix-up over the voters lists on the day of the Ontario election of 1999 reminded voters in that province of the critical importance of accurate, up-to-date lists of voters and of well-trained staff in sufficient numbers to guarantee the smooth operation of an election. Perhaps the most pressing of the outstanding issues needing to be changed is the practice, dating back to the earliest general election in Canada, the Nova Scotia House of Assembly election of 1759, of the cabinet appointing partisans as constituency returning officers. Today the individual responsible for ensuring the application of the terms of the Canada Elections Act, and charged with acting as the representative of the chief electoral officer at the riding level, the returning officer occupies "the single most important post in an election" (Qualter 1970, 144).

The original reason for executive appointment of returning officers was perfectly clear. They "were expected to behave, and often did behave, as agents of the government of the day" (Massicotte 2001, 1). Though the vast majority of returning officers, regardless of their former political allegiances, are now scrupulously fair in their administration of the election and their interpretation of the law, doubts continue to be expressed in some districts about the competence and nonpartisanship of their ROs. Repeated calls by Canada's chief electoral officer and by many of his provincial counterparts to bring an end to a cabinet's selection of returning officers have so far gone unheeded. However, this reform is long overdue.

Changes aimed at bringing Canada's electoral machinery into the era of high-speed Internet and communication technologies took place throughout the last decade of the twentieth century. Elections Canada and provincial agencies all created websites that are easily accessed by the public and, in most cases, frequently updated with election-related news for their jurisdictions. All federal and provincial electoral offices maintain toll-free telephone services year-round. We saw in the previous chapter how Elections Canada was instrumental in the 1990s in getting parliamentary, and to a considerable extent, provincial agreement to construct and maintain a computer-based roll of eligible electors. The decline in voter turnout, so pronounced in Canada in the 1990s (though by no means unique, as dropping turnouts in most other liberal democracies attest), provided the chief electoral officer with the ammunition needed to propose another innovative, technology-based move: Internet voting. At first blush this would seem to make casting ballots more accessible and, as a consequence, seem likely to increase voter turnout. In reality, Internet voting may fall short of addressing the fundamental problem of "who doesn't vote" in elections.

Canada's First Elections

When judged by today's standards of democracy, the first parliamentary elections in the newly confederated Dominion were clearly unacceptable. The process skewed elections in the governing party's favour, openly rewarding supporters of those in office and encouraging corrupt electoral practices by party personnel and voters alike. Bribery of voters and of election officials was not uncommon. There were recorded instances through the mid-1880s of intimidation of voters by political organizers and of election-day violence involving opposing political factions. In all, our early elections were poorly and in many cases corruptly administered.

Until the early twentieth century Canada's elections had several noteworthy features. To begin with, they were highly decentralized. The administration of federal elections was left to the provinces, which meant that voter qualifications, hours of voting, and many of the regulations governing the election of MPs to Ottawa varied from one jurisdiction to another. As the parties in office provincially were often different from the one in office federally, the arbitrariness in the application of the provincial rules and regulations was matched only by its obvious partisanship. The absence of nationally uniform standards fit well with the concept of a highly decentralized federalism that many provincial premiers enthusiastically endorsed, but it was clearly an affront to the concepts of nonpartisanship and fairness as two of the fundamental principles of electoral administration.

Not until 1874 was the secret ballot adopted federally. For the country's first two federal elections (1867 and 1872), balloting was open and public in all provinces save New Brunswick where, from 1855, something billed as a secret ballot had been in use. Open balloting in the other provinces meant a simple verbal declaration to a local election official of the voter's stated candidate preference. In New Brunswick, "The voter merely wrote the name of his choice on a piece of white paper – any piece, and before coming to the poll if he chose – and handed it to the presiding officer" (Ward 1950, 157). As the official was responsible for ensuring the paper had no more than one candidate's name on it, the secrecy of the ballot existed in name only.

The process in all provinces lent itself to corrupt practices. Voters were open to bribery and were held to account by those who had given them money, liquor, or some political favour, if they cast their ballot for a candidate of an opposing party. In a frank admission, one Conservative organizer said elections could not be carried on without money, for "under an open system of voting, you can readily ascertain whether the voter has deceived you" (Ward 1950, 158).

Voting in Canada's first two federal elections took place over an extended period of time. In 1867 it was staggered over six weeks, and in 1872 voting lasted three months. The implications of staggered elections were profound. John A. Macdonald's governing Conservatives, who supported the notion of non-simultaneous elections at the federal level and who, in the prime minister's words, considered simultaneous balloting to be "un-British," benefited from the system in a variety of ways. They tried to time the various local elections to their best advantage. Candidates defeated in an early stage of the election were allowed to run again in the same election in a later contest. Voters owning property in more than one constituency could vote in as many seats as they were qualified. Federal elections in Ontario and Quebec were distinctive in another respect in that both provinces held the vote over a two-day period. Constituency vote totals were taken at the end of the first day and announced publicly, which led to a number of instances of intimidation and bribery of voters during the second-day balloting. Of the provinces, only Nova Scotia held simultaneous elections in all constituencies.

None of the corrupt or blatantly partisan practices of conducting elections in nineteenth-century Canada has survived. An expanding population, a widening franchise, a better informed electorate, and increasingly honest and trustworthy set of election officials eventually combined to make widespread electoral "manipulation and corruption impracticable" (Ward 1950, 277).

A modern election, whether federal or provincial, is held over a twelve- to fourteen-hour period on a single day. Provincial and federal laws provide the detailed framework within which elections are to be conducted, in every case under the watchful eye of a chief electoral officer and his or her staff. Candidates can run in only one constituency at a time, and elected members can sit in no more than one assembly at a time. Electors, regardless of how much property they own in various electoral districts, are entitled to only one vote. Intimidation or bribery of voters, while not inconceivable or unheard of today, is rare and punishable by law. So too are other infringements of the election laws, including campaign financing improprieties by parties or candidates. In these and other respects Canada's election law has in very large measure served to ensure that elections in this country are fairly and honestly administered and are open and accessible to the voters.

Dual-Member Ridings, Infant Parties, and Accommodative Representation

Two other features of Canada's early elections are worthy of comment because of the light that they shed on the concept of representation as Canadians know it today: dual-member ridings and uncontested elections. Both practices played a part in our continued acceptance of the first-past-the-post electoral system and the establishment of centrist, accommodative parties as our principal representational agents.

Two-Member Ridings

The 1867 constitutional provisions creating Canada's first federal constituencies and method of periodic boundary readjustments (ss. 40 and 51 of the British North America Act) explicitly established all but one riding (County of Halifax) as single-member districts. Victoria, British Columbia, soon followed Halifax in electing two members, as did all three of Prince Edward Island's initial seats. Until the practice was ended in 1966, a total of ten federal districts in Canada at some point in their history simultaneously elected two members of Parliament.

Dual-member seats were not unique to Canada. The custom drew on British and North American colonial electoral practices. In Britain the custom could be traced back several centuries to the practice of choosing two knights from the shires and two burgesses from the boroughs to serve in Parliament. For the greater part of the nineteenth century Britain continued to use dual-member seats for elections to Westminster. In the 1860s there were actually more MPs from two-member than from single-member districts in the British Parliament (211 to 196). Following Confederation the provincial assemblies in Canada relied on two-member, or in some instances multimember, seats much more than the federal Parliament. In several of them the practice lasted until the 1970s or 1980s.

Dual-member ridings in Canada were originally seen at the federal level as the answer to a problem of population size in relation to municipal units used as electoral districts. The County of Halifax, for example, was created as a dual-member seat in 1867 because, according to s. 40(3) of the BNA Act, each of Nova Scotia's eighteen counties was to serve as a federal electoral district. With a population roughly twice that of any other county, Halifax was entitled to elect two of the province's nineteen MPs. But a new rationale soon emerged in Halifax, in Prince Edward Island, and elsewhere. Two-member seats presented a way to accommodate a fundamental social cleavage in a locality. Religion was the principal difference that was addressed in this way.

In Halifax, for instance, the two principal religious affiliations were about equal in population. For a century, both the Liberals and Conservatives in Halifax would nominate a Protestant and a Catholic candidate on their two-member slates. This was done in the expectation that support for the party would count for more with the voters than support for two candidates of the same religion. Electors casting their two votes for their party candidates were, in a sense, given a guarantee of simultaneous party representation and a coreligionist in Parliament. The voting record in Halifax throughout the history of two-member elections bore out the expectations of party organizers. "Split-ticket" voting by electors, whereby support was given across party lines to two Catholics or two Protestants, was extremely rare and in itself never affected the outcome of any election. Early on, parties had been accepted as the pre-eminent representational vehicle (Davis 1967).

Two-member ridings were used by parties to accommodate a divisive social variable, to demonstrate to voters that political organizations were capable of brokering social interests, and to ensure the presence in the parliamentary and legislative caucuses of a significant social group that might not otherwise gain much of a legislative presence. In other words, two-member ridings could serve as instruments of social inclusion in the electoral regime. Religion is now a far less divisive feature of Canadian society than it was in the nineteenth and much of the twentieth centuries. Today's list of social cleavages that warrant special representational attention might include language, ethnicity, race, and gender.

Various proposals have been advanced to use two-member ridings to broker contemporary social interests and to enhance the representational presence of groups long underrepresented in elected assemblies. It has been suggested that anglophone and francophone candidates could run as two-member teams where numbers of Canada's official language groups warranted. More recently gender-equal party slates have been suggested as a way to ensure representational parity of men and women in territorial, provincial, or federal assemblies. Candidate lists in two-member seats could also aim at ensuring some measure of ethnic or racial balance on tickets or at assisting geo-graphically dispersed minorities, such as Aboriginals, to gain legislative representation. Whatever the social characteristic singled out for attention by way of dual-member districts, the operative assumption would remain unchanged from the early post-Confederation years: the political party would serve as the critical vehicle for acknowledging important social groupings and for assembling electoral support on their behalf.

Proposals for the establishment of two-member seats have not been without their critics. Opposition to the idea rests largely on representational and practical concerns. A referendum in Nunavut, held only months before that territory was officially created in 1999, defeated a proposal to establish an assembly composed entirely of two-member districts. Each of the ridings would have had an equal number of male and female members and electors would have had to cast two votes to have their ballot counted as valid: one for a male and one for a female candidate of their choice. Following an engaged debate over the concept of representation, the proposal was rejected. Some women's groups, in particular, voiced objections on grounds of tokenism. They saw the idea as an affront to their capacity and ability to win seats in their territorial assembly on their own merits without the assistance of an institutional arrangement.

Critics, particularly at the federal level, have also voiced concern over the effect of two-member seats on the representational role of the elected member. Would male MPs be expected to speak principally or even exclusively on behalf of men, and female MPs only for women? Such an unlikely gender-specific representational notion would be at odds with the traditional view of legislative representation in Canada. Since Confederation, voters and members alike have generally accepted the view that an MP is expected to represent, in the sense of "acting for," *all* of his or her constituents.

If gender or language or race were seen as the social interest to be accommodated through dual-member ridings, the "why them?" criticism would not be long in coming. Why not use such an accommodative mechanism for equal treatment of senior citizens, or immigrants, or some other defined group that could mount a representational claim on its own behalf? Moreover, although the existing direct links between constituents and elected members would continue, the ridings would be twice their current size. The prospect of representing a larger territory, even with a second member to help with that task, would not appeal to those MPs who already speak for geographically large ridings. The new constituency of Kenora, designed by the federal boundary commission in the 2001 census, is almost as large territorially as the entire country of Germany. Any notion of creating an even larger seat in order to establish a dual-member electoral system would almost certainly meet with strong objections in such districts. In all, there is little evident support for the widespread adoption of two-member districts in Canada today. (For more on dual-member ridings in Canada see Courtney 2001, 223-5; Davis 1967; Ward 1967b; and Young 1997.)

Uncontested Elections

Canada's early elections confirmed how tentative and primitive the party system was in the country's formative years. Political alliances were weak and transitory. They resembled factions (and fluid ones at that) more than institutions with their own internal structure and organization. The looseness of the governing alliance was most graphically demonstrated in its defeats on important matters. Between 1867 and 1873, John A. Macdonald's government suffered no fewer than nine major defeats in the House of Commons: five on government bills, two on government resolutions preparatory to bills, and two on resolutions from supply.

That the government continued in office in spite of these setbacks, without a concerted push by the opposition to replace it, demonstrates that the prevailing view of legislative confidence was not what it later became. Also, those on the opposition benches had yet to develop into a cohesive political organization. Indeed, the opposition had had little to do with calling the votes themselves. Of the nine motions on which the government was defeated, six were moved by men normally considered to be its supporters, three of whom later entered Macdonald's cabinet. While Macdonald could generally expect a healthy majority of the House to support him, no legislative vote was safe. Of the 181 MPs in the first Parliament, only 35 did not vote against the government on at least one of the thirty recorded divisions of the 1867-8 session. These are remarkable figures by later standards of intraparty legislative cohesion (Forsey 1963).

In spite of the fluidity of Canada's early party system, the first few post-Confederation years were marked by one notable and lasting organizational and political achievement. Macdonald, who had established an unchallenged title to form the first federal government, put together a loose alliance of seemingly opposite social, linguistic, and religious interests in his Liberal-Conservative party. He brought into his cabinet and, in a larger and no less significant way, his parliamentary caucus, French Canadian ultramontanists, anglophone Montreal commercial and business interests, Upper Canadian Loyalists, and anti-Catholic Orangemen.

Macdonald's was a truly broad coalition of otherwise competing interests drawn from all four of Canada's initial provinces. This "big tent" approach to constructing a winning electoral coalition and, in particular, to using the cabinet as the principal vehicle for brokering regional and social interests, became the model followed by other electorally successful prime ministers. These included, during their most successful periods, Wilfrid Laurier, Mackenzie King, Louis St. Laurent, Pierre Trudeau, and Brian Mulroney. The accommodative approach to forming winning parties was an early attempt to wed inclusiveness, defined here by regional and group interests, with representation. It was to become one of the hallmarks of Canadian party politics.

In a very important respect, Canada's electoral system gave political elites an incentive to build intraparty, interregional coalitions of otherwise diverse social groups. First-past-the-post (FPTP) elections with territorially defined districts encouraged localism in politics. As a consequence, candidates, party organization, fundraising, and much of the electoral machinery needed to run an election have been drawn largely from the locale of the electoral race. Because a party interested in gaining power has to win a majority of the territorially defined seats, FPTP in a country as geographically vast and socially diverse as Canada has encouraged a substantial measure of intraparty accommodation within the historically largest parties. Centrist, big-tent parties become understandable in the context of FPTP. Part of their modus operandi has been to craft inclusive political coalitions large enough to bring them into power.

The infancy of Canada's parties post-Confederation can be measured by the number of uncontested parliamentary elections. Full slates of party candidates were unknown in the early elections, as the Liberals and Conservatives alike nominated candidates in less than 90 percent of the available seats. Moreover, the share of seats won by acclamation in the first three elections ranged between 24 and 26 percent. The 153 constituencies won by acclamation in the elections of 1867, 1872, and 1874 account for 60 percent of all acclamations in Canada's thirty-seven federal elections. An uncontested seat is now clearly a thing of the past. Since 1921, only five MPs have been elected by acclamation, the last in 1957.

The point about acclamation is relevant to understanding why Canada has the FPTP system. At the time of Confederation no other system was considered. This was not because the fathers of Confederation were unfamiliar with other countries, their constitutions, and methods of election. As David Smith has shown, the debates in the Canadian legislatures both before and after the Act of Union of 1841 offer "ample evidence of interest in and knowledge of political happenings in Mexico, Texas, the United States, and Europe, as well as in Britain and the Empire" (Smith 1991, 204). Our constitution makers, like Canadians before and after, tended to think of their institutions in comparative perspective, often basing arguments about their own form of government on "what other countries do." In addition, the works of Thomas Hare, John Stuart Mill (whose *Representative Government* appeared in 1861), and other British proponents of alternative means of electing parliamentary representatives were known to those most involved in crafting the constitutional arrangements of the new Dominion.

Canada's method of electing parliamentarians and provincial legislators was not explicitly discussed in the years leading up to or immediately following Confederation. Instead, the presumption was that FPTP, which had been used for the election of representatives to colonial legislatures, would simply continue for federal and provincial elections. FPTP was appropriate to the political circumstances of the time. There were only two fledgling parties (perhaps, more correctly, one loosely formed governing coalition and one soon-to-be-born opposition party) that between them would split the total votes. Third parties were not on the scene at the time. Moreover, the high proportion of seats won by acclamations in the early years did not encourage consideration of a different, possibly more proportional, electoral system. FPTP was as natural to carry on with after 1867 as, in the familiar words of the BNA Act, the Canadian constitution "was to be Similar in Principle to that of the United Kingdom." Canada's 135-year history of FPTP elections must inform any debate over the future of plurality voting in Canada. The cases for retaining or replacing FPTP will be considered in the following chapters.

Elections Canada

There are two significant dates in the democratization of Canada's electoral system. The first, as we have seen, is 1874 when changes ensuring the secret ballot and simultaneous voting were approved. The second came with the creation of the Office of the Chief Electoral Officer in 1920. Now commonly known as Elections Canada and replicated in a proximate form by all the provinces and territories, this institution has given a legitimacy and a credibility to Canada's electoral process that would otherwise be difficult to match. The establishment of the position of chief electoral officer (who, as an officer of Parliament, reports directly to the House of Commons) was an important breakthrough in the process of making our electoral system more inclusive and responsive to the needs of Canadian voters.

The creation of the Office of the Chief Electoral Officer has to be seen in the context of the events of 1917 and the immediate postwar years. As we know from Chapter 2, at the time of the First World War the Unionist government manipulated the electoral process for its own partisan purpose. The Wartime Elections Act and the Military Voters Act of 1917 proved to be the most controversial pieces of electoral legislation in Canadian history. The acts enfranchised, for that election only, the female relatives of men serving with the Canadian or British armed forces as well as all servicemen. At the same time they disenfranchised conscientious objectors and British subjects naturalized after 1902 who were born in an enemy country or who habitually spoke an enemy language. This legislation was a low point in Canadian electoral history. In 1920, with another election pending, the status quo was clearly no longer acceptable.

Other forces were simultaneously laying the groundwork for substantial changes in the way elections would be run. Various provincial farmers' parties and the Progressives gave strong support to reforms aimed at making the electoral system fairer and more open. The Farmer's Platform of 1916, for example, which was drafted by the Canadian Council of Agriculture and supported by various farm organizations, called for the federal franchise to be based on the provincial franchise as a way of preventing partisan manipulation by federal governments.

As well, the 1921 election would be the first Canadian federal election in which all women twenty-one years of age and older had the right to vote. With such a dramatic expansion in the size of the electorate, organizing elections would become a much larger and more complicated undertaking. One of the many reasons advanced by women's groups supporting the extension of the franchise was that women needed to enter politics to bring an end to abuses of power as well as to clean up the political system. In that context the move to establish an independent, nonpartisan officer to oversee the administration of elections made a good deal of sense. By 1920 public opinion was prepared for substantial changes in the way elections would be managed.

The general electoral officer (the first name given to the chief electoral officer) was, in the words of the minister responsible for introducing the legislation, to "take charge of the election machinery and the conduct of elections in general throughout the Dominion" and, most important, he was to "be in every way a permanent and independent officer" (House of Commons 1920, 1:339). His independence rested on the fact that his "tenure of office" would be the same as that of a superior court judge, meaning that he could not be removed by the government of the day. The strongest selling point of the new legislation was that the officer was to be independent of politics.

The opposition Liberals supported this innovative reform of the electoral system but criticized the government for not going further. Anticipating a common complaint of the decades ahead, they argued that the power to appoint all constituency returning officers should be transferred from the cabinet to the chief electoral officer. The Liberals maintained that the cabinet's continued role in choosing returning officers amounted to the politicians' retaining control over possibly the greatest instrument of political patronage at the local level, although the Liberals did nothing to change the law once they gained office. No government has yet given up that power even though calls by opposition MPs and the chief electoral officer to change the law are repeated regularly.

However, the creation of the position of chief electoral officer (CEO) has helped to enhance the responsiveness and inclusiveness of the Canadian electoral system in other respects. By law, after every election the CEO must present a report to Parliament outlining obstacles to voting and recommending changes to address these problems. The first CEO (Oliver Mowat Biggar) got things off to a good start in his initial report after the 1921 election. He noted that some voters had difficulty participating in the election because they were left off the voters list, and that others, for a variety of reasons, were unable to vote on the particular day selected for the election. Accordingly, he recommended more revision officers to ensure the accuracy of the voters list, and more advance polls to increase the convenience of voting. Parliament adopted both recommendations.

Countless other improvements have been made to the electoral sys-tem as a consequence of a recommendation from the CEO or an initia-tive undertaken by Elections Canada. These include the provision of wheelchair access to polling stations; the use of helicopters to fly in electoral supplies and ballots to small, isolated communities in the North; the provision of assistance in the voting booth for those with a physical disability or impaired vision; and the establishment of polling stations in nursing homes and chronic care facilities. As these examples show, the CEO and his counterparts at the provincial levels have been instrumental in ensuring that the electoral system is responsive to the needs of voters.

The CEO is appointed by a resolution of the House of Commons to hold office without term until age 65. A CEO can be removed only "for cause" by a joint address of both the Commons and the Senate. In the words of the current CEO, the critical role played by the House in the selection process reflects "both the desire for independent decision-making in the various electoral tasks assigned to the CEO over time and the degree to which Parliament identified its own vital interests with the functions performed by the CEO" (Kingsley 2001, 8). It is a given that the person named to the post must be broadly acceptable to the House as a whole. An individual acceptable only to one side of the House would lack the independence essential to endow the head of Elections Canada with the credibility needed to oversee the nonparti-san interpretation, application, and enforcement of the Canada Elec-tions Act.

Two other senior electoral management officials also bring inde-pendence and credibility to the electoral process. The first, the com-missioner of Canada Elections, is responsible for the enforcement of the Canada Elections Act. The official has recently concluded that "most violations of the Act involve minor administrative non-compliance" issues (*Report of the Chief Electoral Officer of Canada* 1997, 85). This stands as an important indicator of healthy democratic elections, for it means that with very few exceptions the parties and candidates, their official agents, the election officials, and the voters respect the terms of the law.

The second, the broadcasting arbitrator, is charged with applying the Act's radio and television broadcasting provisions to the registered parties (eleven at the time of the 2000 election) in a federal election. This responsibility includes apportioning among the parties the broadcast time available for paid advertising and free-time broadcasts, resolving disputes, and creating broadcast guidelines at the start of every election. The time allotted the parties for paid advertisements and free-time broadcasts is based on their respective share of seats and votes in the previous election and on the number of candidates they have nominated in the current election. As the formula clearly favours established parties, the broadcast arbitrator ruled for the 2000 election that statutory factors hindered emerging parties from purchasing the amount of broadcast time necessary to make a meaningful case to the Canadian people (Elections Canada 2000a, 122). To rectify the situation partially, the arbitrator used the discretion granted him under the act to allocate equally among all registered parties the remaining one-third of broadcast time that was not allocated through statutory measures.

One aspect of Elections Canada's work that is little known to Canadians is its considerable involvement in elections throughout the world. Since 1990 it has organized more than three hundred international democratic development missions in some eighty countries around the world. The aim is not to promote Canadian electoral practices or techniques, but rather to help the respective countries select and implement the option that would best suit the country's laws, customs, and environment. Elections Canada's international activities have included providing professional support and technical assistance in areas such as the establishment of electoral district boundaries, the training of election officials, and the preparation of election documents and materials. Advice on various legal and electoral provisions and bilateral exchanges of knowledge and information are common. In developing countries such as South Africa, Namibia, and Haiti (some clearly further along the road to becoming democracies than others), Elections Canada, sometimes through the United Nations, has also served as an election observer to ensure that proper procedures and rules are followed.

Internet Voting

On the heels of the 2000 federal election Canada's chief electoral officer, Jean-Pierre Kingsley, expressed concern about the declining voter turnout that had marked federal and provincial elections through the preceding decade. He was not alone. Citizens, media commentators, academics, and politicians alike voiced their disquiet with the drop in electoral participation in Canada. Barely 61 percent of Canada's registered voters cast their ballot in the 2000 election compared with 75 percent only twelve years earlier. The precipitous decline led a number of election officials, politicians, and political scientists to call for a careful examination of its causes and possible solutions in the hope that the trend could be reversed. Among these proposals were two raised by the chief electoral officer.

Kingsley suggested first that if the participation rates in future federal elections continued to decline it might be necessary for Parliament to introduce compulsory voting. (The case for requiring all citizens to vote in an election will be examined in Chapter 7.) This response to declining voter participation, which Kingsley admitted he found personally "repugnant," gained a wide press and generated some discussion at the time it was made. For the most part, it has since been dropped from any serious consideration of ways to enhance electoral participation. This reflects the absence of support from any party or leading political figures and the strong objections of many Canadians to the idea of being required by the state to vote in an election.

Kingsley also proposed that Internet voting might improve voter participation rates. Although this idea has received surprisingly little attention since he first broached it, Internet voting deserves consideration because of its novelty and the serious challenge it presents to the secrecy and security of the ballot. The chief electoral officer believed that voter turnout would "skyrocket" if all Canadians were able to vote by way of the Internet. An Elections Canada survey had found that 25 percent of Canadians said they would use the Internet if it were available as an alternative to voting at a polling station (Cyber balloting 2002).

Internet voting is an appealing alternative to voting at a polling station because of its ease, convenience, and speed. Voting at home, at a cyber café, or at a specially designed electronic kiosk in a shopping centre, bank, or post office would be an attractive option for many Canadians. The authors of a 1998 report prepared for Elections Canada on the possibility of using new technologies to enhance voter participation concluded that both the telephone and the Internet "offer the prospect of significantly improving the accessibility and the efficiency of the electoral process in Canada" (KPMG/Sussex Circle 1998, 17).

Kingsley acknowledged that the "only impediment" to electors casting an Internet vote in the immediate future was ensuring a totally secure system (Cyber balloting 2002). At a minimum an entirely secure electronic voting system would have to include foolproof protection to guard against hackers, protect the secrecy of the ballot, make certain no one voted more than once, and ensure the votes received via the Internet were cast only by eligible electors. As well, Internet elections would need to provide absolute certainty that a vote cast for one candidate was not counted for another.

The severity of these issues has led a number of computer security specialists to voice serious objections to Internet voting. Their concerns are based on the vulnerability of electronically transmitted information to manipulation in undetectable ways and on a massive scale. The critics see two fundamental problems with electronic voting that together threaten the secrecy of the ballot and the accuracy of the count. The first is the absence of a totally reliable "audit trail" that would enable voters to verify that their votes had been recorded and counted as they had intended. The second is the absence of an electronic ballot box that would verify with absolute certainty the announced vote as an accurate tabulation of all votes cast (Dembart 2003, 1).

Whether those problems can be overcome remains, in the minds of many specialists, an open question at best. Five hundred computer security experts in the United States are so uncertain of the protections offered by currently available voting systems that they have signed a declaration calling for no Internet elections until foolproof measures are in place. It is true that opportunities for electoral fraud and the manipulation of vote totals exist with paper ballots and polling stations. But such fraud could take place only on a much smaller scale than the massive, nationwide interventions that would be possible with electronic voting. In the words of a leading expert on Internet security: "Why are we using eighteenth-century technology to vote in the twenty-first century? Because it works. Twenty-first-century technology is not well suited to elections" (Dembart 2003, 6).

The federal NDP felt sufficiently confident of an Internet voting system developed in the United States that the party allowed electronic voting in the selection of its federal leader in January 2003. Individual party members could cast their vote in one of three ways: at the convention itself, by a mail-in ballot, or through the Internet. In this instance the leadership vote was conducted without any breach of security or other major difficulties with the Internet. However, choosing the leader of the NDP is a far less interesting and difficult challenge to serious electronic hackers than a major national election.

Political parties are often the first to experiment with new electoral technologies. That was case with the "televoting" selections of a decade earlier. Between 1990 and 1994 no fewer than four provincial parties tried a telephone balloting system to choose their leaders. Breaking with the tradition of holding leadership conventions, these provincial parties - Liberals in Nova Scotia, British Columbia, and Alberta and Progressive Conservatives in Saskatchewan - justified the switch on the grounds of greater democracy and increased participation. From their home, office, car, or wherever they happened to be on the day the party leader was to be chosen, registered party electors were able to communicate their leadership preference to a designated number through a Touch-Tone telephone. The record did not conclusively show that the innovative, widely available technology permitted more party supporters to take part in the process. In some provinces the number of participants in the selection process was greater than it would have been at a leadership convention; in others it was not. However, the major obstacle to the new process catching on proved not to be the uncertain level of participation, but the technology itself.

The experiment was clearly premature in that some televoting processes simply did not work properly. In Nova Scotia the Liberals suffered much embarrassment when the provincial party's phone balloting network crashed and the vote had to be delayed by two weeks. The Alberta Liberal Party's system crashed soon after it opened for voting. Not all fees-paying voters were issued personal identification numbers or were able to cast their vote; an unknown number of proxy ballots that were counted may nonetheless have been invalid; and other technical and regulatory problems plagued the vote throughout voting day. These problems brought into question the capability of the system and the ability of party organizers to run the supposedly high-tech system. Interest in Touch-Tone telephone leadership selection has now largely waned in Canada (Courtney 1995, 235-47).

If the technical and security issues of Internet voting can be satisfactorily addressed, the new technology offers the promise of making the electoral system more responsive to the needs of voters. The study commissioned by Elections Canada to examine electronic voting highlighted its accessibility. It was seen as being of particular benefit to "seniors, persons with disabilities, members of ethno-cultural communities, those in isolated communities, and people who are out of the country" (KPMG/Sussex Circle 1998, 17). Electronic methods of voting can be seen, in a sense, as the next logical step in Canada's history of making the ballot more accessible. Advance polls, absentee ballots, extended hours of election-day voting, mail-in-ballots, votes for Canadians temporarily abroad, and other reforms adopted over the years have all shared the goal of making the electoral system "user-friendly" and of helping electors to participate in their most fundamental democratic obligation. If policy makers wish to make the electoral system more responsive to the various lifestyles and circumstances of Canadian voters, then the introduction of Internet balloting that is verifiably secure offers a way of reaching out to voters.

An equally compelling reason offered in support of Internet voting is that it could well increase the participation of young people in the voting process – that is, the very group of eligible voters now least likely to cast a ballot. As André Blais and his colleagues concluded in their latest book in the Canadian Election Study series, "The single most important point to grasp about the decline in turnout since 1988 is that turnout has not declined in the electorate at large, but is largely confined to Canadians born after 1970" (Blais et al. 2002, 46). Many, including Canada's chief electoral officer, believe the Internet would make the act of voting more attractive to our young citizens. Not coincidentally, the largest pocket of support for Internet voting is among Canada's young. Kingsley acknowledged as much when he stated that "youth are raised with Internet technology" (Cyber balloting 2002).

However, false expectations of what Internet voting might accomplish should not be created. It is true that of all the demographic groups, those under twenty-five are most familiar with the Internet. Statistics Canada reported in 2001 that of those between fifteen and twenty-four years of age, 84 percent are familiar with or know how to use the Internet. No other age group has such an impressive figure. The percentages decline with advancing age, until in the final category (those fifty-five and over) only 17 percent are familiar with or are able to use the Internet (Statistics Canada 2001, Table 11).

But familiarity with the Internet is not uniform within specific age groups. It varies largely according to level of education and family or personal income. In Canada in 1999 approximately 19 percent of the lowest quartile income adults had access to the Internet, compared with 71 percent of the highest quartile income group. Similar spreads (30 percent versus 70 percent) are found by contrasting lower with higher education levels (Cuneo 2002, 27-8; Dickinson and Ellison 2000, 7). If we take access as a rough, but not unreasonable, predictor of familiarity with and use of the Internet, there is a "digital divide" in

Canada. Less well-educated and lower-income Canadians do not have the same knowledge of computers and the Internet as their better-educated and higher-income fellow citizens.

These data are even more relevant to the chief electoral officer's assertion that Internet voting would sizably increase the turnout of young Canadians. Like all Canadians, those aged eighteen to twenty-four are divided roughly into two camps. On the one hand are those who are pursuing higher education, have completed a university education, or are in the higher-than-average income bracket. By contrast there are those who are less well educated, have completed no more than primary or some secondary education, or are earning lower-than-average incomes. These are generalizations of two different groups, of course, but for our purposes they will suffice.

Better-educated and higher-income Canadians have a demonstrated tendency to vote. The Canadian Election Study of the 2000 federal election, echoing findings from earlier election surveys in Canada, found the following: "Education is one of the strongest correlates of voting: the more schooling people have, the more likely they are to vote"; "Turnout was almost 50 points higher among university graduates in the youngest age cohort than it was among those who did not complete their high school education"; and "Income proves to be an important determinant of turnout: the higher people's income, the greater their propensity to vote" (Blais et al. 2002, 49-50).

These findings suggest that introducing Internet voting may increase the pool of participants only marginally, if at all. The better-educated young Canadians who already tend to be more likely to vote are also those with a greater familiarity with the Internet. Internet voting in itself may not attract the lower-income and less well-educated voters who tend to be less familiar with the Internet – the very group of citizens least likely to vote. In other words, voting on the Internet could amount to little more than an additional way of casting a ballot for those who already vote and do little to address the more fundamental problem of how to increase the level of voter turnout of young Canadians.

Conclusion

Canada's electoral machinery is, in many respects, second to none. That has not always been the case, as this chapter has demonstrated. The fact that at both the federal and provincial levels the administration of elections is handled as competently and as professionally as it has been speaks volumes about the inherent strength of Canadian democracy. Elections are open, competitive, nonviolent occurrences in this country. They take place every few years and they are conducted without the imposition of arbitrary or discretionary barriers on groups or individuals. Elections are fairly administered and, in a word, accessible to those Canadian citizens who wish to exercise their franchise.

Many of the improvements that have marked the history of electoral administration in Canada have been made with the explicit purpose of ensuring that the electoral system is as inclusive and as accessible as possible. This has clearly been one of the mandates of the various chief electoral officers. Most elections now make ample provisions for enabling handicapped, hospitalized, itinerant, or out-of-country voters to cast their ballots either on election day or in advance polls. Although Internet voting may do little to reach those Canadians who are disengaged from the political system, it nonetheless has the merit of increasing the options for casting a ballot for election participants. Internet voting should be seen as one way to ensure that the system remains open and responsive to the needs of voters, but it should not be held out as an instrument that will induce large numbers of nonparticipants to vote. Whether the Internet will emerge as an alternative means of casting a vote depends entirely on the development of absolute security in the system. Without that guarantee, any move to embrace Internet voting on a large scale in Canada could prove deleterious to an established and healthy electoral apparatus.

CHAPTER 5

- Canada's electoral machinery is now in the hands of professional and nonpartisan officials.
- Canada's federal election process is centralized and uniform.
- Constituency returning officers are partisan appointments made by cabinet.
- Voter turnout is lowest among younger Canadians.

REPRESENTATION, PLURALITY VOTING, AND THE DEMOCRATIC DEFICIT

Unlike countless millions around the world, Canadians today can take pride in their electoral regime. They have a constitutionally entrenched right to vote that the courts, for their part, have resolved to uphold in the most generous of terms. They cast their ballots under the watchful eyes of election officials who are, with only the rarest of exceptions, honest and trustworthy. They know that when the ballots are counted the totals announced are valid. Their geographically defined electoral districts are reconstructed periodically by independent commissions whose mandates instruct them to aim for a measure (in some jurisdictions, a broadly defined measure) of population equality among the districts. Compared with Canada's nineteenth- and early twentieth-century elections and with the current election practices of many other countries, Canada's electoral regime stands up well.

However, one of the core building blocks of Canadian electoral democracy has occasioned considerable, though intermittent, controversy over the years: our method of electing members of Parliament and provincial legislatures. Often referred to as the first-past-the-post (FPTP) method of election (even though there is no "post" for candidates to pass), it could scarcely be simpler. Voters mark a single "X" on their constituency's ballot paper opposite the name of their preferred candidate. The candidate with the largest number of valid votes wins.

If two candidates compete in a riding, obviously the winner is elected by a majority of the votes, but when three or more candidates compete a majority winner is no longer a certainty. As the number of candidates increases, the chances increase that the winner receives nothing more than a plurality of the votes cast.

The FPTP method of election has certain undoubted strengths, but equally some serious faults. These faults have given rise to several calls for replacing plurality voting with a more proportional electoral scheme. The impact that a different method of election might have on our parties and our concept of representation, together with the extent to which the expected benefits of a non-plurality vote system would in fact be realized, warrant consideration.

No analysis of a method of election would be complete without a discussion of representation, for every electoral system is accompanied by at least one theory of representation. Canadians have invoked various concepts of representation from the time of Confederation. The one with the longest history, and which has most heavily influenced our understanding of the relationship between citizens and elected members, is the "trusteeship" theory. Best described by the eighteenth-century English statesman Edmund Burke, this is the notion that elected representatives act as trustees on their constituents' behalf. The twentieth century saw political parties replace individual members as the representational trustees in Parliament. As well, other concepts of representation have surfaced to challenge the trusteeship theory.

Much has been made over the past few years of a so-called democratic deficit in this country. The public and the media have known since at least the early 1990s that deficits in public sector financing should be eliminated. By extension, attacks have been launched on some government institutions, political practices, and policy outcomes on the grounds that they too suffer from a "deficit" - a "democratic" one. The variety of ways in which this term has been employed underscores its utility as a rhetorical device. As we will see, both our method of plurality voting and our concept of representation have been criticized as suffering from a democratic deficit.

Representation in Canada

Like citizens of other democratic states, Canadians attach a variety of different meanings to the term "representation." It is used to characterize elected or appointed agents who have been authorized to act on behalf of others with the expectation that they will be held accountable for their actions. It is also employed as a descriptive device for comparing the linguistic, racial, gender, or occupational composition of an elected assembly with that of the whole population. As well, representation may symbolically embrace myths or images, such as flags and anthems that have developed as part of a political culture. In each of these three respects "representation" applies to an end: actions followed by some measure of political accountability, sociodemographic attributes of the elected and the extent to which these mirror society, and symbolic threads interwoven into a cultural tapestry.

In Canada no single concept of representation has ever been universally accepted. On those relatively rare instances when the question of representational theory has been raised for public discussion, Burke's trusteeship notion of representation has been the most frequently invoked by elected representatives at both the federal and provincial levels. Elected members have explained their, and their parties', actions on issues of public policy by asserting that these have been in "the public's interest" and that they have acted as trustees on behalf of their constituents in determining those policies.

With the Progressives in the 1920s and again more recently with the Reform/Alliance parties, this view of representation has come under attack. Those parties have advanced the claim that elected representatives are not to serve as trustees acting on their constituents' behalf but rather as delegates carrying out their constituents' will. The delegate theory of representation lends support to those voters who want their MPs to vote according to instructions issued by constituents. Adding yet another dimension to the term "representation" are those who maintain that an assembly's democratic legitimacy rests on how exactly its membership approximates the major demographic groupings of the larger society. These competing representational concepts must be outlined before we assess our FPTP electoral system.

The Burkean, or Trusteeship, View

The trusteeship concept of representation was most famously captured in a 1774 speech to the electors of Bristol by the British philosopher and member of Parliament Edmund Burke. Burke expressed no doubts about an elected member's role. When the interests of their constituents approximate their own, members have the responsibility to ensure that the constituents' views are advanced and supported in Parliament. But when their opinions diverge from those of their constituents, elected representatives are under no obligation to follow their constituents' views. Instead, their role as representatives is to act in the larger national interest by exercising their own reasoned judgment about the proper course of action. Burke's celebrated statement about trusteeship is based on the claim that "Parliament is not a congress of ambassadors from different and hostile interests which interests each must maintain ... but a deliberating assembly of one nation, with one interest, that of the whole" (Burke 1996, 69).

It was natural for Canadian parliamentarians of the nineteenth century to be "Burkean" in their approach to representation. A number of them had been born and educated in Britain, where the trusteeship view of representation profoundly affected parliamentary behaviour and party development. Most early Canadian politicians (colonial and post-colonial) were familiar with parliamentary politics, parties, and representation at Westminster. Their natural reference point during legislative debates or political discussions was often the British parliamentary system.

Well over a century later the trusteeship view of representation remains a major thread in the representational fabric in Canada. It is not unusual to see trusteeship representation referred to approvingly in the Commons, provincial legislatures, letters to the editor, and media commentaries. The concept was invoked most recently by the front-runner for the Liberal party leadership, Paul Martin, in the lead-up to the Liberal leadership convention of November 2003. Martin stated his strong opposition to citizen-initiated referendums on questions of public policy. In support of his position he drew on Burke, and argued, according to one account, that Canadian citizens "elect Members to govern [rather than] to implement the febrile will of transitory majorities" (Ibbitson 2002, A4; see also Birch 1971, 78-80; Dawson 1947, ch. 16; Pitkin 1967, inter alia; and Ward 1950, ch. 1).

But the trusteeship model of representation can be questioned on several grounds. Whose interests should the MP consider to be pre-eminent in constituencies with mixed social, cultural, and ethnic populations expressing divergent views about the "right" policies to be adopted? How does the MP's role as trustee square with the fact that, when asked to rank parliamentary responsibilities, members consider the most important to be "helping individuals" in their electoral district, and constituents consider it to be "keeping in touch" with their riding? (Docherty 1997, 190). What role can the MP realistically play in an assembly in which party leadership, cabinet dominance, and government confidence leave little room for independence on the part of elected members? How can voters be expected to know at election time the extent to which their member was individually responsible for the party's accumulated record over the life of the previous Parliament or legislature? Little wonder that one student of Canada's House of Commons has concluded that the Burkean concept of representation is "less powerful" today than it was in Canada's past (Docherty 1997, 143). Parties and party leadership, not individual members, have become the defining institutional vehicles of modern parliamentary representation.

DELEGATED REPRESENTATION

The delegate theory stands in sharp contrast to the trusteeship notion of representation. According to this approach to representation, elected members are obliged to speak, act, and vote on behalf of their constituents. Members are to serve as delegates who have been sent out or commissioned by their constituents to perform a set of tasks that they would otherwise perform themselves. Accordingly, the constituer will is to be expressed by the elected member in the assembly (Pitkin 1967, 112-43).

This approach to representation was embraced early in the twentieth century by the Progressives and the farmers' parties. More recently, the Reform Party of Canada and its successor the Canadian Alliance have publicly subscribed to this view of parliamentary representation. A research study found a measure of public support for delegate representation, although the survey focused only on a single, hypothetical free vote in Parliament on a controversial issue of public policy. Asked how an MP should vote in Parliament on the death penalty, 63 percent (n = 2,316) supported the view that on such a contentious issue MPs should follow the views of those in their riding (Blais and Gidengil 1991, 60-1, 171, and 205).

The delegate theory serves as the basis for recall legislation. Under recall, voters in a constituency can remove their elected member from office when, in the view of those petitioning for the removal, the member has not carried out his or her responsibilities as constituents had been led to expect at the time of the preceding election. The recall of elected members is justified on the grounds that voters, in sizable numbers, can "participate" directly, albeit negatively, in the legislative process. Voters are thus entitled to initiate an action to remove their member from office.

Recall has a spotty and relatively minor history in Canada. At the end of the First World War, the United Farmers movements and the Progressive Party drew on American populism to introduce the idea into the country. The concept found favour in western Canada, where both Manitoba and Alberta experimented briefly with the process. British Columbia is currently the only jurisdiction with recall legislation on its books. It allows for the recall of a member who has held elected office for at least eighteen months after a petition to force a by-election has been signed over a sixty-day period by at least 40 percent of the voters on the constituency electoral list at the previous election. This is an extensive set of hurdles for dissatisfied constituents to overcome.

So far, no member has been removed from office in British Columbia by this electoral tool, but one member did resign from the legislature in anticipation of a successful petition by his constituents. Recall based on undated letters of resignation signed by MPs at the time of their election and available for constituents to employ should they wish to remove a member at some point in the life of a Parliament has been prohibited under federal law since the 1920s. At its core, recall (like the related populist mechanisms, initiatives, plebiscites, and referendums) stands in stark contrast to the older, more pervasive principles of a Westminster-styled parliamentary system, that is, cabinet solidarity and responsible government (Ward 1950, 9-10).

As with the Burkean premise of parliamentary representation, the delegate theory lacks precision and is open to criticism. Which group of constituents warrants having its views on a public policy taken to be pre-eminent by the member as constituting a riding's "will"? Must it be a mathematical majority, and if so how should that be determined? How and by whom are instructions on how to vote in the House to be conveyed to the member? When various issues surface more or less simultaneously on the parliamentary agenda (a not uncommon event) should one viewpoint inform the member of the stand to be taken on the whole package of issues, or is each issue to be dealt with seriatim? The questions surrounding the delegate theory of representation demonstrate that parliamentary representation is not a one-dimensional activity. Burke was one of the first to recognize this.

TERRITORY AND POPULATION

Two representational variables - territory and population - have remained, as we saw in Chapter 3, at the centre of the argument over the design of electoral districts in Canada. The debate over territory and population has formed one of the streams of representational theory in Canada since before Confederation. In 1866 John A. Macdonald offered a simple rationale for low-population, territorially bounded seats. They would ensure that voters, in his words, "had every opportunity of electing men whom they knew" from their own or a nearby community (Macdonald quoted in Schindeler 1969, 88-9).

With much greater social diversity, considerably larger constituency populations, and party-dominated electoral races in every riding in the country, the context within which ridings are constructed is necessarily different today. Even so, the representational questions raised when districts are redrawn remain much the same as in Macdonald's time. Should seats have relatively equal populations regardless of the large districts that would be created in the sparsely populated, often isolated, regions of the country? Or should districts be allowed to vary in population so as to make constituency sizes more manageable in areas with relatively few people, even though urban and metropolitan areas will then have districts with larger-than-average populations?

The continued debate over the weight to be attached to the geographic size of a constituency as opposed to its population cuts across party and regional lines and makes allies, on the one hand, of urban members and, on the other, of rural and northern members. The debate invariably focuses on the different perspective that the various members bring to their representational responsibilities. Those from fast-growing, often ethnically and linguistically diverse urban or suburban districts claim that the difficulties of representing such seats require that they be designed with fewer rather than more people. Those from territorially large districts counter that the amount of time needed to travel to their constituencies and around the isolated communities within them necessitates that their seats have smaller-than-average populations to ensure that they are as geographically compact as possible. Logically, of course, not all seats can be constructed with below-average populations! That is one persuasive reason for ensuring that boundary commissions have the independence and the statutory authority to design seats that in their view best accommodate the conflicting representational demands.

Mirror Representation

Mirror, descriptive, or ascriptive representation draws on the idea that the composition of an assembly should map a society's principal sociodemographic characteristics. According to this view, such variables as gender, race, and language should be reflected as exactly as possible in the membership of the legislature or Parliament. The theoretical underpinning for mirror representation can be traced back to the British Utopians of the early nineteenth century. The concept rests on the premise that elected members who share in common with the larger population a characteristic such as gender, class, occupation, religion, or race therefore typify that group and, accordingly, can "speak for" that group with a unique authority (Birch 1971, 15-18; Judge 1999, ch. 2; Pitkin 1972, 75-6; Swinton 1992).

Mirror representation, though not always by that name, is at the core of the current debate in Canada about the representational deficiencies of elected assemblies. Critics fault FPTP for producing socially and regionally unbalanced party caucuses. Those who draw their electoral ammunition from mirror representation claim that a more proportionate means of converting votes into parliamentary and legislative seats would elect more members from two groups that have traditionally not been present in assemblies in numbers equivalent to their shares of the total population: women and minorities, including Aboriginals.

That claim is one of several in a constitutional challenge to Canada's FPTP system launched in the Ontario Superior Court in 2001 by the Green Party of Canada. Seeking as their remedy a court-ordered suspension of parts of the Canada Elections Act for two years and the adoption by Parliament of a new electoral regime based on some (unspecified) variant of proportional representation, the Greens base a substantial part of their case on the principle of mirror representation. They claim that women and geographically dispersed minorities such as Aboriginals are "far better represented in legislative chambers that elect their members on the principle of proportional representation" (*Russow and Green Party of Canada v. A.G. Canada* 2001, 6.10). As we will see, there is no guarantee that a different method of election would change the demographic composition of Parliament.

Plurality Voting

To get a better understanding of the debate about replacing our method of plurality voting, this section will outline some of the major advantages and disadvantages of FPTP as it has worked in Canada.

Before we look at the pros and cons of plurality voting, three points about methods of election should be understood. Despite being essential to any analysis of electoral systems, these points are often overlooked in the rush to commend or condemn a particular method of voting. The first relates to parties, the second to voters, and the third to institutional transference. All three stem from the fact that every electoral and political system contains its own distinctive elements.

First, political parties find it "rational" to pursue strategies that maximize their chances of converting votes into seats. Because the incentives contained in any method of casting and aggregating votes differ from one electoral system to another, party electoral strategies will also differ according to the perceived incentives present. As mindful as Canada is of its regional, bilingual, and multiracial character, the principal incentive for any party seriously intent on winning sufficient seats in a federal election to form a government is to bridge the regional, linguistic, and racial gaps with policies, leaders, and candidates that appeal to as wide a cross-section of voters as possible.

Second, just as each electoral system provides different incentives to parties and thereby encourages certain electoral strategies, each system enables voters to pursue different strategic options. Voters' strategic choices are influenced by the number of votes they have been allocated, by the way preferences may (or may not) be ordered, and by the manner of distributing (or redistributing) votes among the candidates. Therefore different electoral systems prompt different voting behaviour. Any claim that y number of seats would have been won by a party in a *hypothetical* election under one set of rules, given that it won z share of the votes in an *actual* election under another set of rules, must be treated with suspicion. Just because parties A, B, and C received, for example, 40 percent, 35 percent, and 25 percent respectively of the total popular vote under FPTP does not mean they would have received that level of support under, let us say, some form of proportional representation. Preference ranking among candidates presents the individual voter with choices that are simply not available when a single "X" is all that can be placed on the ballot. This serves to remind us, once again, that institutions, of which electoral systems are among the more visible, affect outcomes.

Third, institutional transference does not take place in a vacuum. Success under one political system cannot be taken at face value to be a sufficient reason for a method of election's adoption in another. Each political system is unique, and the method of election that works in one country may not, in itself, adapt successfully to another. The institutions that would be most affected by a change in election rules would be parties and party and representational systems. More than anything this means that considerable attention must be given to the possible consequences of electoral reform before a voting system is replaced.

With these three aspects of electoral reform in mind, let us examine the two sides of the debate on plurality voting in Canada.

ADVANTAGES OF THE FPTP SYSTEM

FPTP is undoubtedly the easiest electoral system for the voter to use and to understand. Nothing could be much simpler than marking one "X" for a single candidate and counting all the "Xs" at the end of election day to determine the winner. FPTP is also unquestionably the most familiar of all electoral systems to the voters of Canada. With the exception of the alternative vote and single transferable vote systems tried for varying lengths of time between the early 1920s and the late 1950s in Manitoba, Alberta, and British Columbia, FPTP has been used in all federal, provincial, and territorial elections since before 1867. Vote counting is simple and speedy under FPTP. Usually within a few hours after the polls close Canadians know who their new government and opposition will be.

As a rule, Canada's FPTP system has tended to produce single-party majority governments. In the thirty-seven general elections held in

Canada between 1867 and 2000, all but eight brought one party to power with a majority of the Commons' seats. One-party majority governments can be seen as one of the advantages of FPTP, insofar as they imply a greater likelihood of government stability than can be the case where more proportional methods of election have sometimes gone hand-in-hand with coalition governments formed of several parties (in postwar Italy up to 1993, for example). Although not true of every proportional representation system, as a group proportional electoral systems have a demonstrated tendency toward greater government instability, more coalition governments, and shorter periods of time between elections than Canadians have been used to under FPTP.

FPTP in Canada has been particularly favourable to broadly based, accommodative, centrist parties. By winning office with a majority of the seats, a "catch-all" party, as it is called, has generally succeeded in creating a coalition of supporters and MPs drawn from different regions, linguistic groups, ethnocultural groups, and religions. The government draws part of its strength from the fact that it is an *intra-party* coalition. As such, it is less likely to fall apart over controversial or divisive issues than an *interparty* governing coalition formed of a number of parties whose caucuses are each less socially and regionally diverse.

A single-party government's responsibility and accountability to the voters at election time is more likely to be directly established than a coalition government's. FPTP guarantees that each voter casts only one vote in a single-member district – either for or against the government party candidate. When a government has been composed of one party, it is relatively easy for the media and electors to give credit or to assign blame, as they do not have to weigh the competing claims and finger-pointing of a number of parties in a governing coalition. The familiar cry of opposition parties at election time to "throw the rascals out" is easier to accomplish when there is only one set of rascals and the electorate readily understands who they are.

FPTP is based on geographically bounded constituencies each electing a single member. This establishes an obvious, easily understood link between the constituents of a district and "their" MP, as opposed to the more complex representational relationships that result from proportional electoral schemes in multimember districts. Proportionate systems can be faulted for blurring, or even removing entirely, the direct lines of representation that flow naturally from geographically defined identities. Such is the case in Israel and the Netherlands, where the whole country serves as a single district from which all members are elected.

DISADVANTAGES OF THE FPTP SYSTEM

In Canada the principal criticism of FPTP is the seemingly capricious and unfair manner in which it converts the popular vote into parliamentary seats. From the beginning of the movement away from our classic two-party system at the end of the First World War to the recent Parliaments in which five parties have been present, Canadian history contains many examples to support that criticism. Charges of "unfairness" in converting votes into seats have been levelled at Canada's FPTP system for at least three reasons:

1 A party forming a majority government has rarely been elected with the support of a majority of the popular vote. In only three of the twenty-three elections since 1921 (1940, 1958, and 1984) has the party that won a majority of the seats been supported by a majority of the voters. The lowest level of popular support to translate into a majority government came in 1997 when the Liberals won 51.5 percent of the seats with 38.5 percent of the vote.

2 A party forming a government may have received a smaller share of the popular vote but nonetheless have won more seats than its principal competing party. This has happened three times since Confederation: 1957, 1962, and 1979. An added twist to this phenomenon came in 1925 when the Liberal government continued in office in spite of having won both fewer seats and fewer votes than the Conservatives in the election that year.

3 A party winning at least as much if not more of the popular vote as another party may well end up with fewer seats in the Commons.

Again, the 1997 election serves to illustrate the point. The Reform Party of Canada and the Progressive Conservatives were less than one percentage point apart in their total vote (19.4 to 18.8 percent respectively), but Reform elected forty more MPs than the Tories. The Bloc Québécois elected twice as many members as the NDP, but with fewer votes (10.7 to 11.0 percent). Of the five parties electing MPs, the Conservatives won the smallest number of seats in the House in spite of the fact that they gained a larger share of the total popular vote than either the BQ or the NDP.

Judged from the perspective of majoritarian democratic theory, these three points illustrate a perverse tendency of the FPTP system as it has worked in Canada. In converting votes into seats, FPTP can reward regionally strong parties, penalize nationally weak ones, and discriminate against some parties by denying them their "fair" share of seats. Major national and strong regional parties tend to be the principal beneficiaries of the system. All other parties pay an electoral cost by having either too diffuse a support base nationally or too little in the way of regionally concentrated support.

The number and location of seats a party has won often form a misleading and inaccurate portrayal of the actual level of electoral support that it received. For instance, in the 2000 federal election the Alliance party elected two members from Ontario. This implies that that party had gained little support there, whereas in fact almost one in four Ontario voters (23.6 percent) had voted for the party. Changes in party support from one election to the next are often magnified by FPTP as the seat results present a distorted picture of the degree to which electoral support has changed. The most dramatic example is the consecutive federal elections of 1988 and 1993. The Tories' drop in seats from 169 to 2 was far greater than their loss of popular vote, which fell from 43 percent in the first election to 16 percent in the second.

In elections for provincial assemblies, most of which are between one-fifth and one-third the size of the House of Commons, FPTP has produced a few highly distorted results. For example, in New Brunswick in 1987 the Liberals were swept into office by winning every one of the legislature's fifty-eight seats with 60 percent of the vote. In British Columbia in 2001 the Liberals came to power with seventy-seven of the province's seventy-nine seats. In that case, the new government had received 58 percent of the vote.

FPTP's tendency to produce single-party majority governments may be seen as a drawback of the system. Some favour a coalition government that includes representatives from two or more parties, arguing that a multiparty government represents a larger cross-section of society. As a result a coalition forces compromise among more regionally, linguistically, or culturally uniform parties.

FPTP does not take a voter's preference orderings into account. In the extreme, this limitation can lead to perverse results. For example, a constituency's least preferred candidate may be elected because voters are limited to a single choice. Assume thirteen voters and three candidates:

Five voters have the preference ordering A B C.
Four voters have the preference ordering B C A.
Four voters have the preference ordering C B A.

A plurality vote elects A even though eight of the thirteen voters prefer B to A and eight of the thirteen prefer C to A.

Women and Aboriginals have never gained seats in the House of Commons commensurate with their share of the total Canadian population. Although the 1997 election saw the election of a record sixty-two women MPs, and although at 20.6 percent of the total membership, this figure represented the highest percentage of women elected in any country using FPTP, it nonetheless falls far short of equal gender representation in the House. The same is true of Aboriginal Canadians. Their share of the total population is approximately 3.5 percent, but in 1997, when a record five Aboriginal members were elected, they captured only 1.7 percent of the seats in the House.

As outlined above, the advantages and disadvantages of FPTP present two contrasting pictures of our method of election. FPTP is seen, on the one hand, as an easy to use, familiar electoral system that provides a considerable measure of government stability. It is favoured by those who want to ensure reasonably clear lines of accountability and responsibility at election time. FPTP and territorially defined electoral districts go hand-in-hand in Canada, with the consequence that parties seriously intent on gaining office have been denied the opportunity of constructing their electoral base solely on the support of a single region or sociodemographic group.

On the other hand, FPTP is faulted for exacerbating regional tensions and for having denied some regions and many voters a "voice" in Parliament or around the cabinet table. The classic attack on FPTP by Alan Cairns paints a picture of a method of election that distorts party representation in Parliament to such an extent that the "sectional cleavages" among the parties tend to be "much more pronounced in Parliament than they were at the level of the electorate" (Cairns 1968, 61). Added to that, using the language of mirror representation, is the obvious fact that women, Aboriginals, and ethnic minorities are under-represented in Parliament. Judged by strict majoritarian principles, FPTP has failed the test more often than it has passed, if the passing grade is determined by the number of occasions governments have been elected by a majority of the popular vote. The various faults of FPTP are seen to be serious enough that they form part of the argument that Canada is experiencing a democratic deficit.

The Democratic Deficit

It is now much in vogue in Canada to speak of a "democratic deficit" in this country. The term has been used widely over the past few years by politicians, editorialists and media reporters, academics, and members of the public. What is striking about the term, apart from its alliteration, is its imprecise definition, which lends it to multiple uses. To say a governmental institution, or a practical or conventional political arrangement, is suffering from a democratic deficit casts the process(es) by which its decisions were reached in an unfavourable light. To criticize public policies as the consequence of a democratic deficit is to impute a negative evaluation either of the arrangements followed to adopt them or of their content and presumed impact on society.

The various ways in which "democratic deficit" has been used in recent years in Canada demonstrate how supple the term is. Campaigning for the leadership of the Liberal Party of Canada, Paul Martin referred in several of his speeches to a democratic deficit in Parliament. By this he meant the tight executive controls over backbench MPs that had become a hallmark of the Chrétien years. Others use the term to fault executive federalism for its "eleven men in suits" approach to resolving important constitutional issues and for creating a gap between the electorate and those holding public office. Democracy Watch, a citizens' advocacy group based in Ottawa, has criticized party fundraising practices and the powerful links between lobbyists and politicians on the grounds of contributing to the democratic deficit. It is also said that growing pubic cynicism about Canadian politics and the sharp decline in voter participation rates are evidence of a growing disconnect between the public and the politicians. That disconnect is claimed to be part of our current democratic deficit.

One of the academic critics of Paul Martin's view of a democratic deficit argued that the former cabinet minister and putative prime minister was preoccupied with intraparliamentary reform at the expense of electoral reform:

> Mr. Martin does not mention the democratic deficit caused by the Canadian system of translating votes into seats that routinely returns majority governments with a minority of the popular vote, that disenfranchises Canadians who vote for parties that run on issues that cut across regional divides, that returns as members individuals who receive a minority of the votes cast, and that is associated with a low representation in legislatures of women and racial minorities (Cameron 2002, A19).

For those who see reform of the voting system as leading to a more engaged citizenry and to assemblies that more precisely mirror Canadian society, it seems clear that switching methods of election could reduce the democratic deficit. To these reformers, replacing plurality voting with a more proportionate electoral scheme holds out the promise of reversing the decline in voter turnout and of increasing the number of women and minorities in Parliament (Rebick 2001).

Plurality Voting, Representation, and Canadian Democracy

Debate over electoral reform in Canada has been episodic. It has not followed a consistently upward-moving trend line growing in intensity from one election to the next. The issue all but disappears from public view when, as in 1968 and 1984, elections produce majority governments whose level of popular support and level of parliamentary representation are not wildly incommensurate, the governing party enjoys a measure of electoral and parliamentary support from all regions, and the opposition parties see their respective share of votes more or less reflected in their share of seats.

Interest in reforming the electoral system reignites whenever the regions sense a heightened alienation from the centre and find comfort in pointing at the plurality electoral system as a contributor to that alienation, and when the Commons seats of the parties bear an odd relationship to their respective share of popular votes. Those conditions describe the last three federal elections, in 1993, 1997, and 2000. Whether the interest in electoral reform is sustained beyond the next few elections remains an open question. It is too early to know whether the elections from 1993 to 2000 were transitional, in the sense of ushering in a party system that will remain fundamentally different in number and character from that of the past, or simply aberrational, in the sense of being followed by something approximating the party system from the late 1950s to the early 1990s. (An analysis of the breakdown of Canada's former party system and its possible, but as yet uncertain, replacement with a new one, is found in Carty, Cross, and Young 2000.)

Although there was a spirited debate in the House of Commons in 2003 on an opposition member's motion to hold a national referendum on proportional representation (defeated in the House by a vote of 144 to 76), the intensity of and interest in the current debate over the continuation of plurality voting has yet to match that of the 1920s. That was when the question of reforming the electoral system was first addressed. Following several debates and votes that cut across party lines in 1923, calls to replace FPTP were rejected in the House of Commons. The provinces of Manitoba and Alberta joined the electoral reform bandwagon in the 1920s when they replaced plurality voting with the alternative vote (AV) and the single transferable vote (STV), only to return to plurality voting thirty years later for many of the same reasons that they had adopted proportional representation in the first place. (For a discussion of the strengths and weaknesses of AV and STV see Courtney 1999b, 10, and Mair 1986, 292-307; for an account of Manitoba's adoption and subsequent abandonment of AV and STV see Courtney 2001, 36-44.)

Several books and journal articles, together with a large number of newspaper columns, have been devoted to electoral reform over the past few years. The great majority of these have called for the replacement of plurality voting by some variant of proportional representation. Several conferences sponsored by major public policy institutes have been held on electoral reform. Websites, electoral reform organizations such as Fair Vote Canada, and Internet chat groups have been created to encourage public discussion of the topic. A year after the court challenge launched against FPTP in 2001 by the Green Party of Canada, the Law Commission of Canada released a discussion paper on electoral reform. Four provinces (New Brunswick, Prince Edward Island, Quebec, and British Columbia) have established committees to explore alternative electoral systems and the mechanics of moving away from plurality voting. Other provinces, notably Ontario, may soon follow suit. The considerable interest in the subject bodes well for Canadian democracy and indicates a serious attempt to debate the concerns about plurality voting expressed by members of the public, a number of academics, and some politicians.

Yet those who favour electoral reform in Canada agree neither on a preferred alternative to FPTP nor on the benefits expected to result from a changed method of voting once it is in place. The electoral systems proposed so far have included AV, STV, **two-round** elections, **mixed-member proportional**, and, in a few cases, strict proportional representation. As these systems differ substantially, in any future examination of voting methods they must be judged according to their suitability to democratic governance and representation in Canada. Chapter 7 will return to this question.

Without an agreed-upon alternative to plurality voting, much of the debate over electoral reform in Canada is played out in a kind of political and constitutional limbo. "What if we had proportional representation?" has become a standard opening line among speechmakers and writers setting out to capture their readers' attention on the matter of electoral reform. What *kind* of proportional representation is often left unsaid, and if one of the four or five principal alternatives to plurality voting is advanced the accompanying explanation often fails to explore both side of the issue fully. The possible disadvantages of replacing the plurality vote with a different form of voting are rarely presented alongside the presumed advantages. Yet both the potential costs and benefits of change to the political and representational systems deserve to become part of the debate.

A complicated relationship exists between institutional change and presumed outcomes. Therefore caution is urged on two fronts with respect to the presumed benefits of electoral reform. These are the *expectations* that might be created about what electoral reform can accomplish, and the possible *impact* that electoral reform could have on our parties, our representative system, and governance.

WILL THE EXPECTATIONS BE REALIZED?

There is a divergence of opinion over the objectives to be served by changing the method of election. To some the principal benefit of adopting a preferential ballot, for example, would be to unite the votes of those to the right of the political spectrum. The argument is that with alternative voting the Liberal hegemony in federal elections would be more likely to be brought to an end. To others the major gain from electoral reforms would be a reinvigoration of the political system and, ultimately, an increase in the number of electors turning out to vote. To still others the assemblies elected under a proportional scheme would better reflect the gender and racial composition of society at large. How certain are any of these expectations to be met under a different electoral system?

A United Electorate to the Right of Centre

Some believe that if Canada were to replace FPTP with a form of preferential voting such as AV, whereby voters could rank their district candidates from most to least preferred, then the calls to "Unite the Right" would at last be met. That certainly has been the hope of those who over the past few years have searched for a way of combining the votes of parties to the right of centre in an attempt to defeat the federal Liberals. Their argument has been that the Reform/Alliance party and the Progressive Conservatives have split the "anti-Liberal" vote in recent federal elections and that a different method of election would reverse the trend. They reason that if voters could cast preferential ballots, those who would give their first choice to the Alliance would choose the Tories as their second option and those who would give their first choice to the Tories would choose the Alliance candidate as their second option. Through the gradual elimination of lower-ranked candidates and the transfer of ballots from one candidate to another, Alliance and Tory candidates would fare better than they have under FPTP and could, conceivably, win enough seats between them to replace the Liberals with a coalition government.

The difficulty with this proposition is that it almost certainly would not come to pass. From the Canadian Election Studies of the 1993, 1997, and 2000 elections we know that Alliance voters preferred the Conservatives to the Liberals as their second choice. In the 2000 election, for example, Alliance supporters' second-choice preferences favoured the Conservatives to the Liberals by 38 percent to 27 percent. But the reverse was far from true of Conservative supporters. For their second choice Tory voters picked the Liberals over the Alliance by a margin of better than two-and-a-half to one: 45 to 17 percent. Alliance, as it turned out, was the second choice of very few voters, only 9 percent in the country as a whole. This contrasted with the Tories who, at 40 percent, were the second choice of more voters than any other party (Blais et al. 2002, 76-7). These data suggest that a proportional scheme could not be counted on to consolidate the "right of centre" vote.

Higher Levels of Voter Turnout

On the face of it, the case for an increased level of citizen interest in politics and voter participation under proportional elections makes a good deal of sense. If electors support a candidate or party that is clearly going to lose, or so certain to win that an "extra" vote would be unnecessary, the value of a single vote can easily be cast into doubt. In those situations, voter turnout could reasonably be expected to decline. Conversely, levels of voter interest and turnout should go up when the "utility" of the vote is seen as greater. Under a scheme in which a party's share of seats reflected in some measure its share of votes, each individual vote could be perceived as more determinative of the final outcome. Thus, parties would have an incentive to encourage their own supporters to participate and voters would have less reason not to vote. One study found that, all other things being equal, voter turnout tended to be roughly 7 percent higher in countries with some form of proportional representation than in those with plurality voting (Blais and Carty 1990).

The problem, however, is that all other things are not always equal. It is not possible to predict in which direction voter turnout will go following electoral reform. This is demonstrated by the experiences of two Westminster-styled parliamentary jurisdictions that moved from plurality voting to a proportional scheme. The first example draws from the comparative electoral history of Manitoba and Saskatchewan over the past eighty years, and the second from New Zealand's experience since 1996 with a mixed proportional/plurality electoral scheme. Neither of these cases confirms that an increase in turnout under proportional elections is necessarily a "done deal."

Over the course of its thirty-five-year history with AV and STV (1920-55), Manitoba experienced a sharp drop from its previous levels of voter turnout. Prior to the introduction of preferential voting, Manitoba's voter turnout averaged 82 percent. Under AV and STV, when governing coalitions became the norm and the number of acclamations over the course of nine elections reached sixteen in 1941 and fifteen in 1949, voter turnout slumped by about one-quarter to 63 percent. Since the return to FPTP, average turnout has reversed slightly to 68.5 percent (n = 13 elections).

By contrast, in Saskatchewan (with many social and economic similarities to Manitoba) the nascent party system in the early years of the twentieth century prompted far less voter participation than the province's later, highly competitive two- and three-party elections. Prior to the provincial election of 1921, voter turnout in Saskatchewan averaged 67 percent. This was 15 percentage points below Manitoba's participation rate for the same period. But during the period in which Manitoba experimented with proportional representation, Saskatchewan's turnout jumped to 79 percent, an average that disguises the fact that for seven of those nine elections (1921-56), the range was between 80 and 85 percent. Voter turnout figures in Saskatchewan have since averaged close to the 80 percent level (n = 12 elections), and no candidates have been elected by acclamation since three were acclaimed in 1925.

These figures suggest different party development patterns in the two provinces, which can in part be explained by how parties maximized their strategic opportunities under the respective electoral systems. In Manitoba from 1922 to 1958, the Progressives were never out of office. They were the central player in the formation of every government, whether it was coalition or single party. Until the return to true party competition in the late 1950s, there was a reduced level of interparty rivalry and a heightened tendency to nonpartisanship in the province as a whole. Both of those features of Manitoba's party system led to reduced voter interest and partisanship, which ultimately contributed to the decline in voter turnout (Donnelly 1957, 20-32). Voters in such a context might have asked, why bother voting if the results are relatively easy to predict in advance, if the major governing party never changes, and if the incremental value of one vote will likely make little or no difference to the outcome?

In Saskatchewan, by contrast, the party system has been highly competitive following its early formative years, and the shares of votes of the two principal parties much closer to one another than was ever the case in Manitoba under AV and STV. Saskatchewan's system can best be described as a competitive two-party one, although the two parties have changed over time (the list has included the Liberals, Conservatives, CCF, NDP, and Saskatchewan Party). In eight decades no candidate has been elected by acclamation to the provincial legislature, the last Independent candidate to be elected was in 1948, and voter turnout has averaged 10 to 15 percentage points more than Manitoba's. In that period seven governments have been defeated in an election, with the principal opposition party at that point taking over as the new government.

The contrasting experiences of these two provinces was later repeated by New Zealand's experience with voter turnout after its switch in the 1990s from FPTP to mixed-member proportional (MMP) elections. In 1993 New Zealanders agreed through a referendum to replace their plurality vote system with their own variant of the MMP scheme, in which roughly one-half of the assembly's members would be elected from single-member districts and the other half from party lists according to a party's share of the national vote. It was anticipated, in the words of the royal commission whose report served as the basis for the change, that "a turnout higher than under plurality" would result from MMP elections (Royal Commission on the Electoral System 1986, 56-7). That justification for moving away from FPTP was echoed by the media and throughout the debate leading up to the adoption of the new electoral system.

The reverse, in fact, has proved to be the case. The turnout level in the first MMP election (1996) was 78 percent. Although this level was a slight improvement over the previous two FPTP elections (1990 and 1993), it nonetheless fell far short of the roughly 85 percent average under plurality voting of the previous seventy-five years. From 78 percent in 1996, to 75 percent in 1999, and 72 percent in 2002, New Zealand's voter turnout has now declined to its lowest level in the country's history. (A different way of measuring voter turnout in New Zealand confirms the same phenomenon. It shows a 15 percentage point drop in participation rates from an average of 92 percent throughout the 1980s to 77 percent in 2002). One expert on the impact of electoral change in New Zealand has concluded that the decline in voter turnout is a direct result of weaker party identifications and reduced party campaign contacts with voters under MMP (Vowles 2002, 599; turnout figures from Vowles 2002, 588-9; LeDuc and Pammett 2003, 2; and the University of Auckland's New Zealand Election Study data, provided to the author 29 October 2002).

The voter differences in Manitoba, Saskatchewan, and New Zealand cannot be explained solely on the grounds of electoral systems. Cultural, representational, social, and political variables are all at play here in what is ultimately a complex matter. Voter turnout is itself a function of many variables, only one of which is an elector's perceived value of an incremental vote or the true level of interparty competitiveness in an election. Nonetheless, these examples demonstrate the complexity of the question of electoral reform and confirm that changes in methods of election cannot be certain of attaining anticipated goals.

Greater Electoral Success for Women and Minorities

Electoral reform advocates in Canada expect that the distribution by gender and race of those elected to Parliament and legislatures would change under a more proportional voting scheme. The Green Party, for example, in its Charter challenge to FPTP, said that it favoured a method of election other than plurality voting so that women and minorities, including Aboriginals, would be elected in larger numbers to Parliament. Indeed, some comparative studies of methods of election confirm a positive link between proportional elections and increased election of females (Rule 1994).

The election of relatively few women and Aboriginals to Parliament cannot be laid entirely at the feet of FPTP. As we know, both groups were late in getting the franchise and the right to run for public office: 1920 in the case of women, 1950 for the Inuit, and 1960 for status Indians. As well, although changes have been made in recent years, intra-party structures at the federal, provincial, and local levels were in the past overwhelmingly the preserve of white men. This, in turn, reduced a party's capacity or willingness to recruit female and Native candidates for public office. Women and Aboriginals have fared far less well in gaining party nominations than non-Aboriginal men and, accordingly, have been underrepresented on the ballots. When they have been nominated, members of both groups, particularly women, have often had to run in seats that are from their party's standpoint more difficult, if not impossible, to win.

Of course, none of these hurdles is totally independent of the method of election, which as we learned earlier affects parties' strategic behaviour. Nonetheless it would be a mistake to conclude that the fault line in mirror representation has stemmed exclusively or even largely from plurality voting. Cultural, historical, and institutional norms and practices must also form a part of the explanation.

Some studies support the claim that one way to correct for representational imbalances of women in legislative assemblies is to replace FPTP with a more proportional method of election. According to one authority, list PR (list proportional representation, in which voters in multimember districts accept either a party's set ordering of candidates or indicate their own preferences within a single party's list or among lists of the various parties) offers the most "woman-friendly" electoral system (Rule 1994). Political parties in a proportional system are claimed to have more incentive to produce a "balanced ticket" than in plurality elections (Bogdanor 1984, 113-14). Parties have an opportunity to appeal to the greatest number of voters by putting forth lists containing a demographically and socially wide cross-section of society. Thus, so the argument goes, women and minorities would be positioned high enough on a party's list to ensure their election in greater numbers than would be the case under FPTP.

The difficulty with the generalized proposition that PR systems lead to greater female and minority representation is that not all parties or countries use PR elections to promote a greater measure of "mirror representation" in their assemblies. The likelihood of women gaining legislative seats under list PR is well established in Sweden, Denmark, Finland, Norway, Netherlands, and Iceland. These countries rank highest in the world for the share of women in their parliaments. They are followed by Germany and New Zealand, two countries whose MMP electoral systems offer some of the same incentives as list PR for parties to construct diversified lists of candidates. But compare such other list PR countries as Israel (ranked 47th in number of female legislators), Greece (77th), and Brazil (95th), or a modified-MMP country such as Italy (68th), or STV countries such as Ireland (54th) and Malta (73rd). Despite their more proportional electoral systems they all fall well behind countries like Canada (26th) and the United Kingdom (33rd) that currently use FPTP (Inter-Parliamentary Union 2001, 1-5).

How do we account for the differences? History and political culture help to answer that question. Women were given the vote and played a significant role in public affairs in the Nordic countries far before most other Western democracies. Women's political socialization in Scandinavia thus stands in stark contrast to the experience of women elsewhere. Moreover, gender quotas were established either by the states or the parties to guarantee the election of a predetermined share of women in local and parliamentary elections (Bystydzienski 1994, 62; Bystydzienski 1995, 20; Zimmerman 1994, 4-10). Canadian lawmakers have eschewed setting fixed quotas on grounds of gender and race. So too have the parties, with rare exceptions such as the federal NDP in the occasional recent election. Should governments or parties wish to impose such quotas, FPTP offers no institutional impediment. Quotas may be more difficult to institute in single-member districts than in list or MMP systems, but PR is not an absolute necessity for affirmative action policies on candidate nominations.

The representation of any group in an assembly is the result of a complex mix of institutional variables, perceived electoral incentives, political strategies, and cultural norms. The six countries at the top of the list of female parliamentarians share a number of distinctive features. They are all developed, territorially small northern states with a history of women playing an important part in public affairs well before that was true elsewhere. Although it shares many similarities with them, Canada is vastly different from Sweden, Denmark, Finland, Norway, Netherlands, and Iceland. Our country is a territorially vast, multicultural, officially bilingual, and ethnically diverse federation with a unique representational and party history. The complexity of our interrelated representational, party, and electoral systems must not be overlooked in any comparison with the electoral experience of other countries.

POSSIBLE IMPACT

As noted earlier, political parties have different incentives to win seats under different rules of election. With few exceptions, since Confederation Canada's major "brokerage" parties have sought to accommodate major social and regional differences. For the better part of Canadian history coalitions have been built *within* Canadian parties rather than *among* them, reflecting an incentive contained in FPTP for more or less centrist, mainstream parties interested in minimizing interregional and interlinguistic conflicts.

The same incentives for parties to broker social cleavages are not necessarily present in other electoral systems. In the Canadian context, a PR electoral scheme could prompt parties intent on gaining office to discontinue appealing to that area of the country in which they have been weakest. Most of the current parliamentary parties (with the obvious exception of the Bloc Québécois) could reasonably expect to get a few (perhaps no more than one or two) members elected in their weaker regions. Consequently parties could conclude that their optimal strategy would be to concentrate on winning additional support in their areas of electoral strength rather than to deploy resources in their areas of weakness.

Adopting such a strategy could, in turn, bring into question the appropriateness of continuing accommodative, brokerage-style campaigns. Strategists could argue that their party's principal area of electoral weakness had been "taken care of" by the PR method of election and their resources would be better deployed where they would be expected to have greater effect; that is, where the party had demonstrated strength. There is no certainty that this would happen under PR, of course, but it is conceivable that a proportional scheme would diminish the ability of political leaders to persuade colleagues, supporters, and voters of the need to display the political equivalent of the military victor's greatest attribute – continued goodwill to the vanquished. Because Canada's social, regional, and linguistic diversity lends itself to accommodative politics and brokerage parties, changing to a highly proportional election system could have a profoundly negative impact on national unity. (Concerns about the possible implications of electoral reform for Canada's national parties are addressed more fully in Courtney 1980 and 1999b.)

Conclusion

The central question on Canada's electoral reform agenda in the early years of the twenty-first century involves our method of plurality voting. The push to replace FPTP with some more proportionate electoral scheme is a direct result of the fallout from the last three federal elections and two or three very lopsided provincial ones. Between 1993 and 2000 voter turnout declined steadily, a five-party Parliament became the norm, a government with a majority of the Commons' seats but fewer (sometimes substantially fewer) than a majority of the votes was elected, and the four opposition parties had oddly mismatched shares of seats and votes. In terms simply of majoritarian democratic theory the election results were found wanting.

Most politicians and citizens have yet to become engaged in the debate over reforming the method of election. A handful of interested citizens, some of the national and local media, several political scientists, and a few public policy institutes have taken up the cause. To them, FPTP is fundamentally flawed. It has been faulted for skewing results in such a way as to deny voters a voice in the assembly roughly in proportion to how they had voted; for having worked against the electoral prospects of women, minorities, and Aboriginals; for having reduced the incentive to vote to the point where electoral participation figures have become a concern; and for having exacerbated the regional cleavages in this country.

These are serious charges deserving full, informed, and reasoned discussion in the years ahead about the social, regional, and representational costs of plurality voting. To be balanced, however, the discussion must also look at the implications of a different method of election for individual citizens. Would Canadian democracy be truly enhanced by electoral reform, or would the changes amount to little more than institutional tinkering with no assurance to the electorate of real "value added" to their political system? As no institutional change is ever neutral, the likely effects of electoral change deserve to be understood as fully as possible before changes are made.

Part of the argument in favour of replacing FPTP is similar to the arguments made earlier in support of expanding the franchise and reforming the boundary readjustment process. Those changes were justified on grounds either of inclusiveness or responsiveness. The gradual expansion of the franchise was undertaken to make the electoral system more *inclusive* of Canadian citizens and to treat all Canadians equally. Control over the design of electoral boundaries was relinquished by the politicians as a *response* to the long-expressed criticisms of the public and the media. The partisanship of the district readjustment process violated standards of democratic fairness and impartiality.

In spite of that similarity, granting the right to vote to previously non-franchised groups and transferring the power to determine the size and shape of electoral districts to arm's-length commissions were reforms that carried with them something that by definition is missing in the debate over the electoral system. The consequences of the earlier reforms were *known* in *advance*. Groups targeted for inclusion in a widened franchise (men without property, women, Asian Canadians, Aboriginals, and so on) were identified clearly as the intended beneficiaries of the reform. That was true as well of changes in the electoral boundary readjustment process. By transferring the power to draw boundaries to independent commissioners, the reform delivered, as expected, a needed legitimacy to an otherwise tarnished political process and led to the construction of ridings with a greater measure of population equality. But a changed method of election cannot be assured of delivering a specific set of benefits. The comparative record demonstrates there is no absolute certainty that the anticipated objectives of electoral reform will be met.

If the method of election were changed, parties and voters would be given the opportunity of employing different strategic options from what they had under FPTP. On the face of it, incentives seem to exist under PR that do not under FPTP to increase voter participation, party inclusiveness, and system responsiveness in elections. Some form of proportional voting might give political parties a huge incentive to mobilize as wide and as varied an electorate as possible; that is, to be as inclusive of the population as possible. The logic is simple: a party's share of the vote determines its share of the legislative seats. For their part, voters might be given the incentive to vote because they have an interest in ensuring that their preferred party gets as large a share of the votes as possible in order to gain as many seats (Denmark 1998).

That proposition is logical, but expectations about what would occur once an electoral system is changed in the direction of proportionality are sometimes turned upside down. We saw that with respect to voter turnout in both New Zealand and Manitoba. Other factors and considerations muddy the electoral waters between expectation and reality. These include, but are not limited to, party competition, the possibility that the process of coalition formation under a more proportional system is unresponsive to public preferences, weaker party identifications, and reduced direct party campaign contacts with voters. The fact remains that electoral reform can promise a good deal. Much of this promise may be deliverable, such as the possibility of a greater sense of voter efficacy or of greater public trust in an electoral system that is seen to convert votes into seats in a fairer manner. But equally at least part of the promise may be unrealizable and may, in turn, lead to public disaffection with politics over unmet expectations.

CHAPTER 6

- First-past-the-post voting tends to elect one-party majority governments.
- FPTP is a familiar electoral system that helps to ensure considerable government stability.
- FPTP has a demonstrated tendency to convert votes into seats in a seemingly capricious manner.
- FPTP makes it easier for regionally strong parties to elect MPs but harder for nationally weak parties.

7 AUDITING CANADA'S ELECTORAL SYSTEM

At the federal, provincial, and territorial levels the Canadian electoral regimes of the early twenty-first century are in almost all respects vastly different from those of the nineteenth century. The franchise laws are now clearly more uniform and inclusive than those of the nineteenth century. The blatant partisanship that once defined the boundary readjustment processes has given way to an arm's-length procedure that encourages public participation. Electoral offices in all jurisdictions have responded to individual and group pressures for more accessible and user-friendly voting arrangements. The professionalism and independence with which officials administer elections gives voters the confidence that their secret ballot is precisely that, and that at the end of election day the counting of ballots will be honest and fair to all concerned. These are all marks of a mature electoral democracy.

There are, to be sure, troubling episodes that quite understandably capture media and public attention when they occur. They serve to remind us of the vulnerability of electoral arrangements. Occasionally ballot boxes have been known to go missing and never been located. Election night ballot counts in a constituency have sometimes been in error. Judicial recounts, however rare they may be, have decided in favour of a candidate other than the one mistakenly declared winner on election night. Election officials, as in the Ontario provincial election of 1999, may have been too few in number in some polls or too ill prepared to manage the process without delays and subsequent complaints from voters. Accusations of partisanship on the part of election officials at the riding level, while extremely rare, have been made from time to time. Such was the case, for example, in Quebec at the time of the 1995 provincial referendum. However uncommon these sorts of episodes may be in the management of elections in Canada, they underscore the care, preparation, and vigilance needed to oversee elections. On balance, Canadian voters can be confident that they are getting that vigilance.

The franchise, electoral districting, and election administration are the three building blocks that meet the tests of acceptability in our democratic system. This list could well be joined by the new method of registering voters once it has been established with absolute certainty that the continuously updated electoral roll is as complete a list and is as well understood by voters as the door-to-door enumeration it replaced. To this end, the new voter registration system may have to be modified. For reasons of inclusiveness, accuracy, and familiarizing the electorate with the Register, periodic interelection enumerations may have to supplement the electronically based list. We learned in Chapter 3 that the two methods of registering voters have been fused successfully in some other jurisdictions. In Canada, door-to-door enumerations could be conducted automatically three years after every federal election. They would serve as the principal source of changes needed to update the data file as well as the state's way of informing voters about their registration and their entitlement to vote.

The one building block that has not been substantially altered since Confederation is, of course, our method of election. Plurality voting in the early twenty-first century is not fundamentally different from in the nineteenth century. Voters cast a single "X" and the winner is the candidate capturing more votes than any other. It is that simple. The debate now under way about the appropriateness of first-past-the-post voting to modern Canada is profoundly important. Plurality voting may have the great strength of being uncomplicated and of making it easy to distinguish winners from losers, but the list of complaints about FPTP stands as a challenge to the system's place in a democratic regime. In an era of five-party politics, FPTP based on territorially designed districts is faulted for restricting voter choice to a single option; making it difficult for non-regionally based groups to mount credible campaigns for public office; translating vote shares into seats inequitably among the parties; and leaving voters who are disaffected with the system little option but to drop out.

Those are formidable criticisms. However, as will be argued in this chapter, any debate over the future of plurality voting must involve broader democratic theory. When we speak of participation, inclusiveness, and responsiveness, we are using terms that resonate with citizens and that give them some sense of what to look for in an electoral regime that labels itself "democratic." The Supreme Court of Canada has drawn those terms forcefully to our attention through its interpretation of the franchise in Canada. But additional aspects of a democracy bear upon any consideration of electoral reforms. In Canada's case these clearly include a complex weave of customs, assumptions, laws, and constitutional principles that have evolved with time. As well, the method of election should not be assessed in isolation from our representational practices or from the political parties that serve as the institutions charged with aggregating votes and forming governments. Governance and representation must be at the heart of any assessment of electoral systems.

As has been noted throughout this book, voter turnout has been on a steady downward slope in recent federal and provincial elections and, in the view of several observers, has reached worryingly low levels. Some critics of FPTP point to plurality voting as a major contributor to declining voter participation. Yet the thirty-five-year contrasting experiences of Manitoba, using AV and STV, and Saskatchewan, using FPTP, suggests that the explanation for declining voter turnout lies elsewhere. Certainly Canada is not alone among Western democracies to have experienced declining levels of voter turnout over the past decade. Even countries that changed their method of election during the 1990s in part to encourage voter participation, such as New

Zealand with its move to a mixed-member proportional system, have witnessed dropping voter turnout over the past decade.

One possible remedy that has occasionally been debated in Canada is to make voting compulsory. This chapter looks at the arguments presented in support of and in opposition to a legal requirement that all eligible citizens *must* vote. Would Canadians accept this solution to reverse the slide in voter turnout? Following our examination of compulsory voting, and based on our analysis of the electoral building blocks examined in this book, we will try to determine what social and political variables must be met before an electoral institution can change. This should help us to understand better why our franchise, electoral districting, voter registration, and electoral machinery have all undergone massive changes since Confederation and why our plurality vote system has so far remained unchanged.

Compulsory Voting

The subject of compulsory voting in Canada has been broached recently by, among others, the country's chief electoral officer and some newspaper columnists. Their argument has a compelling, yet simple, logic. Turnout is slipping, and that has serious implications for the quality of government, the legitimacy of elections, and Canadian democracy. In the words of two advocates of compulsory voting, Andrew Coyne of the *National Post* and Jeffrey Simpson of the *Globe and Mail,* "the fact that fewer and fewer people are involved contributes to the increasing vacuity of our elections" (Coyne 2000) and "the sharp decline in voting reflects a general disengagement from the democratic process" (Simpson 2002). As well, the rationale for compulsory voting draws in part on the view that citizens, having been given the right to vote, ought to exercise it - even if that means coercive action by the state.

The case for compulsory voting rests upon a mixture of philosophical and pragmatic considerations. Citizens have been recognized as having a right to vote; therefore the state has the responsibility to ensure that that right is exercised. It is claimed that for those elections in which turnout levels are high, the assemblies that are elected and the legislation that is adopted have a greater legitimacy than those in which fewer citizens vote. Elections held with compulsory voting are said to prompt greater citizen awareness of issues and policies and to serve as important educational tools for the citizenry. Advocates of compulsory voting note that levels of voter turnout are higher (sometimes markedly so) in compulsory voting countries than in those where voting is voluntary, although they admit that levels of spoiled ballots and of voters refusing to accept their ballot from election officials are also higher.

Two more pragmatic considerations are also offered in support of compulsory voting. First, individuals are required by the state to do all sorts of things they might otherwise choose not to do, yet for the general interest of the individual and the larger population the state enforces these obligations. For example, laws require compulsory education up to a certain age, payment of taxes owed, the wearing of seat belts in moving vehicles, and (in some countries) military service. Andrew Coyne (2000) extends that argument by asking, "What's the big deal if you have to vote as well?" Second, political parties find the idea of compulsory voting attractive because the task of mobilizing voters at election time (to which parties in countries with discretionary voting devote considerable time and resources) is off-loaded onto the state. Freed of that responsibility, parties and candidates are then able to concentrate their entire efforts on the campaign.

There are, not surprisingly, critics of the whole notion of compulsory voting. Some object to the possibly substantial administrative and judicial costs incurred by the state to enforce the legislation. Others argue that if voting is a right, so too not voting is a right. By exercising the option to abstain from voting the elector has made a deliberate choice to boycott an election. Although some people are simply too lazy or unwilling to take the time or make the effort to vote, others may have profoundly important reasons for not voting. They may find the local candidates or the political parties unacceptable, or they may disagree fundamentally with the issues on which a campaign has been waged.

Canadian supporters of compulsory voting point to Australia as the model of compulsory voting that Canada should emulate. Other countries have mandatory voting (notably Belgium for over a century now), but Canadians look to Australia for several reasons, as we saw in Chapter 3 in learning about the shift away from partisan boundary redistributions to independent commissions. Both countries are economically advanced, territorially large federations whose political systems have been shaped by their Westminster-style parliaments. Both countries have relatively small populations whose location patterns and movements share striking similarities. Sparsely populated regions cover vast land areas, and the continuing rural exodus and considerable post-Second World War immigration have combined to increase markedly the populations of the major metropolitan centres of each country.

Concerned about the drop in voter turnout to levels as low as 47 percent, Australia adopted compulsory voting for federal elections in 1924. Australian citizens who do not vote are subject to a fine (ranging between A$20 and A$50) if they are unable to present an acceptable excuse to election officials or a court. The country now records electoral participation rates among the highest in the world. Expressed as a share of the total registered electorate, voter turnout has hovered around the 95 percent level for the past several decades. But near-universal electoral participation comes at a price. Most Australians see the requirement as a manifestation of what electoral democracy entails. Nonetheless, some object to being required to do something they would prefer not do. Disgruntled citizens who might otherwise choose not to vote opt to "fulfill" their obligation by deliberately casting spoiled ballots. Over the past few decades an average of 3 to 4 percent of the ballots has been spoiled in each election in Australia. This compares with less than 1 percent in Canada.

Canadians see the issue differently. There are no recent surveys on the question of compulsory voting in this country, which in itself may indicate how little interest there is in the subject. Even so, on those rare occasions that the topic is broached among members of the public, media commentators, academics, and political science students, opinion is split. Some, like the Australians, support the argument about increasing turnout and balancing democratic rights with responsibilities. An equal, or possibly larger, body of opinion argues against this on the lines of classical liberal theory. In their view the state should play no part in serving as a watchdog of electoral participation. Voting is seen as an individual, not a community, decision, and the value of the vote would therefore be diminished if individuals under threat of prosecution were forced to fulfill an unwanted obligation.

The arguments on both sides of the issue are powerful and get to the heart of the democratic theory of elections. Australians see compulsory voting as an important element of their democracy. Rights carry responsibilities, they fervently believe, and therefore the state should be empowered to ensure that those responsibilities are carried out. Many Canadians dismiss compulsory voting as an affront to what they consider to be a fundamental democratic principle, the right not to vote if one so chooses. Is one country right and one wrong? Not at all. Both Australia and Canada have a profound attachment to democratic values and institutions. The relative weight that each country attaches to the principle of participation, however, is a study in contrasts.

Strikingly, these two parliamentary and federal democracies, each with an embedded tradition of accepting open public debate over alternative parties and leaders in the heat of an election campaign, demonstrate the different interpretations that can be attached to a principle at the core of electoral democracy. Australia's state-enforced commitment to compulsory voting places far greater emphasis on the value of the participation variable of democracy than is true in Canada. For its part, Canada to date has demonstrated a greater acceptance of a laissez-faire attitude in its elections. Voter registration is not statutorily required of Canadian citizens, nor is voting. The Canadian approach to participation, which is shared by most other Western liberal democracies, rests on the notion that the state has no legitimate role to play in enforcing democratic participation by its citizens. As a concept that is at the heart of governance in both Australia and Canada, "democracy" lends itself to the deployment of different arguments in support of fundamentally divergent views of the respective obligations of the state and its citizens.

Is it the role of the state to require its citizens to participate in an election, at least to the extent of voting on election day? Does the fact that individuals enjoy the right to vote endow the state with an equal right to ensure that a citizen's responsibility is fulfilled and that as large a share as possible of the electorate votes? These questions are not easily answered, for they raise issues of rights, responsibilities, and authority. Canadians have so far been loath to introduce the compulsory vote in either federal or provincial elections on grounds of interfering with an individual's freedom of choice. For the foreseeable future that seems the appropriate course for Canada to continue. In the absence of compelling evidence that there is a serious drop in voter turnout that can best be addressed by mandatory voting and that voters accept the need for state-enforced electoral participation laws, the choice of whether or not to vote is best left to individual Canadians.

Reforming Electoral Building Blocks

Our comparison of the five building blocks of Canada's electoral system (the franchise, constituency redistributions, electoral machinery, voter registration, and method of voting) has found that the first three were changed at different stages of Canadian history largely in response to public pressures or changing social attitudes. These were, especially in the case of the franchise and redistributions, bottom-up reforms that gradually percolated from the populace to the policymakers. The principal source for the changes to the fourth building block, voter registration, came from a different direction. The continuous electoral roll replaced door-to-door enumeration as an elite, or top-down, response to an institutional arrangement that was seen as no longer adequate to the task. The fifth of our building blocks, the plurality vote system, remains largely unchanged from pre-Confederation Canada. This raises a question: what are the preconditions for reform of an electoral institution? To answer that question let us draw up a list of the conditions that would have to be in place before some other method of election could supplant Canada's plurality electoral system.

BOTTOM-UP OR TOP-DOWN?

A basic and obvious condition for the reform of any representational building block is that elected officials, particularly governing elites, must accept the case for modifying it. Currently there is no evidence of any measurable level of support for electoral reform among Canada's governing elites at the federal level. Such reform proposals as have been made have come from MPs on the opposition benches or parties without elected members, such as the Greens. The probability of a federal government accepting the need for changes at the present time is low, for based on the experience to date with FPTP a different method of voting would not likely work to the advantage of a party already in office or a party poised to win under FPTP. With few exceptions parties gaining office benefit from plurality voting, an axiom that is unlikely to change. A government's electoral self-interest will weigh heavily in any reform of electoral institutions.

That said, a series of unstable, possibly coalition or minority single-party governments in which minor parties successfully bargained for electoral reform might lead to sufficient inter-elite political pressure for electoral reform to force a government's hands. Alternatively, as in New Zealand in the early 1990s, profound public dissatisfaction with and disdain for politicians and parties, following on the heels of an influential and respected commission of inquiry examining alternative electoral methods and recommending its preferred choice, could be the catalyst needed to prompt the principal political actors to accept changes to the electoral system.

Neither of these alternatives is currently in the works in Canada at the federal level, for several reasons. The majority Liberal government, notably its leadership and party membership, shows no serious interest in electoral reform. Likewise, there are few Canadian equivalents to New Zealand's "agenda-setting" public interest groups on electoral reform, which gained widespread public attention and support. More important, public dissatisfaction with the electoral system and politicians has yet to reach the level of intensity that it did a little more than a decade ago in New Zealand.

Canada's Royal Commission on Electoral Reform (the Lortie Commission) was neither asked nor did it choose to consider alternative electoral methods. Without a recommendation from an influential and high-profile commission calling for a changed method of election, the case for reform becomes harder to construct. If a continuing and manifestly general dissatisfaction with plurality voting were present amongst the Canadian electorate, and if there were widespread agreement on a single alternative espoused by a respected national commission of inquiry, it would be easier for electoral reformers to fashion a coalition supportive of changes to the voting system. Such conditions would properly lead to genuine and far-reaching demands for electoral reform that, based on the experience of New Zealand, those in government would ignore at their peril.

Is the case for electoral reform as compelling when the principal arguments for reform derive from periodic or intermittent dissatisfaction from a limited number of individuals (academics, some opposition MPs and media commentators, and a few citizen advocacy groups) with the results of a particular election or set of elections? Without extensive, sustained, and profound disapproval on the part of the electorate with the current system, coupled with general agreement on an acceptable alternative to plurality voting, the push for electoral reform in Canada is likely to fall on deaf government ears. Given the abundance of alternative proposals recently bandied about in Canada, ranging from mixed-member proportional through alternative vote, two-round, and single transferable vote, to two-member constituency plurality vote elections, widespread agreement at the federal level on a single preferred option to the current system does not currently exist.

Federalism

Our current plurality vote system works through two institutional and territorially bounded filters. The first is the single-member electoral district, examined in Chapter 3. The second is federalism. Both constitute important representational institutions for the periodic reallocation of federal seats among the provinces, the designing of district boundaries, the aggregating of votes, and the eventual determination of election winners and losers. How, if at all, does federalism figure in electoral reform?

A comparative study of electoral systems in advanced democracies has concluded that Canada is not naturally predisposed to electoral reform because of the complex interrelationship between the federal system, single-member districts, and the geographical distribution of citizens by language groups. Unlike a number of other countries, Canada's principal social cleavage (language) is not distributed more or less evenly across the country. Ours is a territorially large federation in which the two principal linguistic groups are geographically concentrated - francophones predominantly in Quebec and anglophones predominantly in all other parts of the country. Even distribution would serve as a powerful inducement to replace plurality voting with a more proportionate electoral scheme designed to protect the linguistic minority and to guarantee it a measure of representation at the federal level. However, as it stands the geographic distribution of the two dominant language groups and the federalized institutional structure within which their electoral choices are aggregated collectively lend no support to the case for a reformed electoral system at the federal level (Boix 1999).

An extension of these findings to the intraprovincial distribution of linguistic minorities leads to the same conclusion with respect to elections to the Commons. Anglophones in Quebec and francophones in New Brunswick, Ontario, and Manitoba are present in sufficiently large numbers and are sufficiently concentrated in particular areas that they have long commanded a majority of the population of several federal electoral districts. Consequently they have elected MPs in numbers roughly proportionate to their share of their province's population and have held control of, among other things, the local branches of national parties.

The importance of that control cannot be minimized. It has been reflected in the demonstrated ability of linguistic minorities to dominate the nomination process and to elect MPs from their own language group. Were their numbers evenly distributed around a province rather than being concentrated in certain areas, a linguistic minority might then find grounds to press for a more proportional electoral scheme. That is not now the case. (The impact of the geographic concentration of minorities on electoral districting and on electoral outcomes is discussed further in Courtney 2001, 137-44.)

Federalism may encourage electoral reform through role modelling and institutional transference. In Chapter 3 we saw that following the acceptance of independent boundary commissions in Manitoba, the reform gradually extended to the rest of Canada. The investigations into plurality voting now under way in Prince Edward Island, Quebec, and British Columbia may eventually lead to changes to the method of voting in those three provinces. The moves those provinces make on the electoral reform front will be closely watched elsewhere. It is important to remember, however, that institutional transference did not occur after Alberta and Manitoba switched to transferable voting in the 1920s even though there was far greater political support for a similar move at the federal level than is now the case. Apart from those two provinces and, briefly, British Columbia in the 1950s, no other jurisdictions have ever replaced their plurality vote system. All three Western provinces eventually reverted to FPTP.

More relevant than past history to the possibility of provincial-to-federal institutional transference, however, is the fact that provincial elections are contested in jurisdictions that are considerably different from the federal one and by fewer parties, of whom several have no counterpart at the federal level. Provinces are smaller in area and population, have a less socially heterogeneous mix of voters, and elect legislative assemblies with substantially fewer members than is the case federally. Given the tendency of FPTP to inflate the share of seats of the winning party and deflate the share of seats of the losing parties relative to their respective shares of votes, the net effect of these differences has been to produce a few wildly lopsided provincial legislatures. Clean sweeps or near clean sweeps (all but two or three seats) of the legislatures have been recorded in New Brunswick, Prince Edward Island, Alberta, and British Columbia. It is not surprising that some of these provinces have appointed bodies to look into changing their method of election.

To summarize the points being made about reform of this electoral building block, Table 7.1 highlights the principal conditions or variables that need to be successfully met before the federal electoral system could be changed to some as yet undetermined, non-plurality voting system and the extent to which they are currently present. In the case of reforms to the franchise, boundary readjustment process, electoral administration, and voter registration, clearly the support of

Table 7.1

Reforming a representational building block: First past the post

Variables	Present to what extent?
Support for change from:	
Media	Moderate but intermittent
Public	Low to moderate but intermittent
Academics	Several supportive of change
Commissions	No support from Lortie Commission
Public interest groups	Some active groups
Government agencies	Elections Canada not proactive to date
Courts	None
Elected officials	Low on government side; moderate in opposition parties
Agreement on the alternative	No, although numerous alternatives proposed
Resources on which to draw	Some academic research, mostly pro-reform
	No influential pro-reform commissions of inquiry at the federal level
Obstacles	Politicians' self-interest
	Public ambivalence
	Unease about implications for government stability
	Complexity of issue compared to familiarity of FPTP
Impact of federalism	Negative in terms of concentration of linguistic minorities
	Positive if provincial test tubes are created and institutions are transferred

governing elites and the agreement on a single alternative to the current system were essential. They are the sine qua non of electoral reform. Government leaders play the vital constitutional and decision-making role on such questions. Without elite support and a substantial measure of public pressure for a change in our electoral arrangements, no change will be forthcoming. That is also the case with respect to the possibility of compulsory voting in Canada, which is currently a non-issue with the public and the politicians. In sum, given the absence of a single alternative strongly favoured by an electorate seriously disaffected with plurality voting and the failure to date of governing elites to embrace the cause of electoral reform, the chances of adoption of a reformed electoral system at the federal are low at present.

Democracy and Electoral Reform

No electoral system is neutral. We have seen how in Canada the current franchise laws distinguish among residents of this country according to age and citizenship. District boundaries help to create communities of interest different from those that would have been created had the lines been drawn another way. Voter registration systems vary in their ability to capture eligible electors. How the method of voting converts votes into seats affects the composition of governing institutions, the concept of representation, the number and type of political parties, and, ultimately, the content of public policies. In the final analysis, how the institutions of our electoral system are configured directly affects our understanding of democracy.

As we learned in Chapter 5, Canadian political leaders never debated which method of election they would adopt for the new Dominion. It was entirely natural for them to continue with a familiar electoral system, even though proposals for alternative electoral arrangements were being debated in other parts of the world at the time of Confederation. As a consequence, plurality voting has roots in this country that are now well over a century old, older if colonial elections are included. So too do our constitutional, federal, and parliamentary systems have deep roots. Collectively all of these institutions are the source of our machinery of government and are at the heart of our democratic system. Accordingly, they have helped shape our political culture, the understanding that the electorate has about our political processes and parliamentary government, the internal organizational and authority structures of our parties, and our representational system. It follows that the fundamental principle that should guide any search for a different method of election is that whatever alternative is eventually settled upon must be compatible with our constitutional, federal, parliamentary, and representational systems.

At their most basic levels, the parliamentary and federal systems have served since Confederation as the institutional frameworks within which parties have developed and electoral outcomes have been determined. Barring some major and unforeseen event, that will continue to be the case well into the future. Within those parliamentary and federal arrangements, the problems of plurality elections in Canada that are typically identified by observers for special comment derive from the degrees of "fairness" and "representativeness" of electoral outcomes for parties, voters, and regions. Those terms cast a wide net. They range from concerns expressed by Alan Cairns more than three decades ago about the tendency of our electoral system to produce sectionalized and potentially non-integrationist federal cabinets and parliamentary caucuses, to the more recent attacks on grounds of democratic theory about the "unfairness" of FPTP to some regions, parties, and voters.

Two aspects of Canadian democracy should inform any quest for a new method of election: governance and representation. On the matter of governance, a different electoral method must ensure the continuation of certain fundamental cornerstones of our parliamentary system. This should hold true even though coalition governments of two or more parties become the governing norm as a consequence of electoral reform. What are Canada's essential constitutional principles? At their most basic level they include cabinet secrecy and solidarity,

Commons confidence votes on issues of critical public policy, responsible government, and (however shop worn this concept may have become) individual ministerial responsibility. Regardless of the changes that may be made to the electoral system, these constitutional and parliamentary pillars of Canada's political system should be neither fundamentally altered nor discarded in favour of some as yet untried and unfamiliar ones.

On the representational side, the range of considerations is no less important, though they are, in a sense, more complex. The advent of identity politics, in which women, Aboriginals, and ethnocultural groups have made powerful representational claims, has the potential to make electoral reform a particularly salient issue for some of those who now feel disadvantaged by plurality voting. The move toward direct democracy has also helped to reshape representational practices. The appeal of such plebiscitary vehicles as referendums, recall, initiatives, and, in the case of national and provincial party organizations, universal membership votes, has been unmistakable. The creation of the Reform and then of the Alliance parties demonstrates that appeal.

Identity politics and direct democracy can be expected to harm the age-old accommodative model of Canadian parties if parties see a different electoral system as offering a different set of strategic options that work to their advantage and if they choose to fashion their respective support bases around a narrow range of social, linguistic, racial, or regionally concentrated supporters. Electoral changes could mean the demise of the transnational brokerage party model first crafted by Macdonald and Laurier. New institutional arrangements bring with them new incentives and strategic options. For truly national parties intent on winning office under the plurality system, the most obvious of these strategies has been to create and maintain the "big tent" within which interregional, linguistic, and social differences are accommodated. Whatever reforms are introduced to Canada's electoral system should not encourage parties to abandon that option in order to pursue other more narrowly or sectorally based ones.

To be sure, electoral democracy is about participation, inclusiveness, and responsiveness. Those, after all, are the concepts within which we have explored the five building blocks of Canadian elections. It stands to reason that the value attached to any individual vote will be determined according to how frequently and under what conditions citizens participate, how inclusive the system is of its citizenry, and how responsive governments are to their demands and expectations.

But elections in a democratic system are also fundamentally about who will govern us for the next three or four years. In Joseph Schumpeter's words, "In a democracy ... the primary function of the elector's vote is to produce government" (Schumpeter 1962, 273; see also Aucoin and Smith 1997, 31). Elections are about ensuring *responsibility* by governments for their actions and *accountability* by governments to the electorate. If the electoral machinery has been properly fashioned, if the building blocks have been correctly constructed, if the concept of representation and the party system are suitable to a society no matter how diverse, regionalized, and scattered it may be, responsibility and accountability will follow logically and elections will be judged democratic.

It is not hard to find faults with electoral systems on grounds of both governance and representation. The faults differ, of course, both in kind and magnitude from one system to another. What is critical in any evaluation of the costs and benefits of moving from one method of election to another is to know where the trade-offs will have to be made. As Canadians begin seriously debating alternative electoral systems in the years ahead, the long-term implications of change for both governance and intraparty representational practices must remain central to their analysis.

Chapter 7

- The Canadian electoral system has historically responded to public pressures and changing social attitudes.

- Australians see compulsory voting as an important element in their democratic system. Canadians do not.

- Changes to Canada's electoral system must be compatible with our parliamentary, federal, and constitutional systems.

Discussion Questions

Chapter 1: The Rules of the Electoral Game

1 Should an assessment of Canada's electoral system include "building blocks" other than the five identified in Chapter 1? If so, what are they? Why should they be included?

2 Do you accept the definition in Chapter 1 of elections in free and democratic societies as distinguished from those in nondemocratic regimes? Are there other variables that ought to be included in that definition as well? If so, what are they?

3 For an electoral system to be judged truly democratic, a useful theoretical framework must first be constructed whereby the judgment can eventually be made. What elements of such a theory not present in Chapter 1 would you wish to see included?

Chapter 2: Who Can Vote?

1 Should the voting age be lowered to sixteen? Seventeen? Fully consider the arguments in favour of retaining the current eighteen-year-old level and in favour of lowering it by a year or two.

2 Should Canadian citizens resident abroad for an indefinite period of time be entitled to vote in Canadian elections?

3 Should questions about who is entitled to vote be resolved by the courts or by Parliament?

4 Should some citizens lose their right to vote? Consider convicts, Canadians living abroad, and those who have demonstrated a tendency over several elections not to vote.

5 What are the advantages and disadvantages of provinces having different electoral laws and regulations from those at the federal level?

6 Compare the qualifications for voting in the nineteenth century to those we currently use. What events and attitudes have caused this shift?

Chapter 3: From Gerrymandering to Independence

1 Should Canada employ a strict "one person, one vote" system similar to that in the United States?

2 Would non-territorially defined electoral districts be preferable to territorially defined ones?

3 How much significance should be attached to "communities of interest" in establishing electoral districts?

4 What changes to the electoral district boundary system would increase political participation in public hearings?

5 Should "affirmative gerrymandering" aimed at improving Aboriginal and minority representation in elected assemblies become a fundamental principle of electoral redistributions?

6 Should either of the senatorial or grandfather clauses be changed or abandoned? What are the advantages and disadvantages of each?

Chapter 4: Registering Voters

1 It is possible to retain the National Register of Electors and conduct campaigns that would be longer by a week or so than their present thirty-six-day minimum. Would there be merit in doing so?

2 Should the onus for registration be on voters or on the government? How does each coincide with Canadian democratic theory?

3 What advantages, if any, does the new form of voter registration provide over door-to-door enumeration?

4 How important is cost when it comes to registering voters? Should expenses be subordinate to registering a maximum number of voters or not?

5 Is shortening campaign time a legitimate concern? If so, why? What impact would shorter campaigns have?

6 How important is "human contact" when it comes to registering voters? Will the absence of face-to-face contact under the new registration system detract from the ability to mobilize voters?

Chapter 5: Electoral Machinery

1 Should two-member ridings be adopted for elections to Parliament and provincial elections?

2 Some argue that two-member ridings in federal elections could provide for increased representation of various minority groups such as women and Natives. Explore the various arguments for and against such a system.

3 Should Internet voting be introduced for federal and provincial elections? Would such a change end declining voter participation rates?   p 110 - 111

4 Newly emerging democracies in many parts of the world look to countries like Canada to provide assistance in organizing and administering elections that are open, fair, and accessible. What aspects of Canada's election machinery lend themselves to being easily exported and to being of greatest utility to countries with little or no history of democratic elections? p118

5　In what respects are Canada's current electoral machinery and electoral administration most improved since Confederation? What major problems or issues of electoral administration remain to be addressed?

6　Given Canada's decreasing rate of voter turnout, can any changes be made to the country's electoral machinery that could increase voter participation?

Chapter 6: Representation, Plurality Voting, and the Democratic Deficit

1　What are the advantages and disadvantages of the first-past-the-post system?

2　Should Canada employ a voting system that ensures a majority winner? Would you consider a different voting system preferable? Why?

3　What are the advantages and disadvantages of plurality voting systems as compared to proportional voting systems?

4　Would the advantages of reforming our method of voting outweigh the disadvantages? Why?

5　Would proportional representation increase voter participation and ensure the election of more women, minorities, and Aboriginals in Canada?

Chapter 7: Auditing Canada's Electoral System

1　Should voting be compulsory? If voting is a right, is it not also a responsibility that government should require its citizens to fulfill?

2　What democratic trade-offs would a system of compulsory voting introduce to Canada?

3　What factors have to be in place for institutional reform to come about in our electoral system?

4　How does federalism figure in electoral reform? What would be the implications for parties if some provinces changed their method of election and other provinces and the federal government did not?

5　What obstacles to adopting a different method of election do you think could be overcome most easily?

Appendix: Three Challenges and Possible Reforms

Allocation of House of Commons Seats among Provinces

CHALLENGE

Commons seats are redistributed every ten years. The number of electoral districts awarded the provinces is determined by the Constitution Act, 1982, which guarantees that no province shall have fewer MPs than it has senators, and the Electoral Boundaries Readjustment Act, 1985, which ensures that all provinces will receive the same number of seats as they had in 1976 or in the 1984-8 Parliament, whichever is less. Given the continuous shifts in population that have been captured in the past several decennial censuses, these two provisions have led to an increasing divergence among the provinces in their average population per district. The post-2001 redistribution highlights more than any previous one the population variations among provinces. The combined average population per seat in Ontario, British Columbia, and Alberta is 107,477; for Prince Edward Island, Saskatchewan, and New Brunswick it is 58,900. Calls for greater equality of population in federal districts can be expected in future from those who argue that the "electoral value" of the votes of Canadians varies according to which province they happen to live in.

REFORM

This challenge does not lend itself to an easy solution. There is little likelihood that the senatorial floor guarantee will be dropped or changed, for the constitutional amending formula requires unanimous federal and provincial agreement. The best hope therefore lies in reform of the grandfather clause. The Lortie Commission presented a sensible proposal for ending grandfathered seats through the gradual elimination of one seat per decade for those provinces currently protected by that provision. With time this would reduce, though clearly not eliminate, the interprovincial population variance.

Appointment of Returning Officers for Federal Electoral Districts

CHALLENGE

Described as the person occupying "the single most important post in an election" (Qualter 1970, 144), the returning officer (RO) is crucial to the impartial and competent administration of an election at the local level. Individuals named to that post in each of Canada's 308 ridings are, with few exceptions, political appointees of the governing party. To their credit ROs have, again with few exceptions, carried out their assigned responsibilities without partisan favour or major incident. Nonetheless the appointment procedure, which dates back centuries to the time of blatant partisanship in electoral administration, leaves much to be desired in terms of modern, democratic theory and practice.

REFORM

In regular reports to Parliament the chief electoral officer has called for an end to cabinet appointments of ROs. To fill the positions he has proposed instead an open, advertised competition run by Elections Canada. This would be an improvement over the current practice.

National Register of Electors

CHALLENGE

Having replaced the familiar door-to-door enumeration with a so-called permanent registry of electors, Elections Canada needs now to address an issue that existed on a far more modest scale under the previous system. The new electronically maintained, continually updated, and centrally located list is only as reliable as the data supplied to it. Those data include information on changes of address, deaths, additions, and changes of names. In the first election under the new registry (2000) the 301 ridings collectively handled more than 3.6 million revisions to the lists presented to them by Elections Canada only thirty-six days before. This was nearly three times the 1.3 million revisions made in 1997. There is, as well, some evidence to suggest that the 2000 list of electors may have been slightly less complete than the lists compiled under door-to-door enumeration.

REFORM

If the new Register is to be as current and complete as possible at the time of an election, biennial or triennial door-to-door enumerations should be introduced. The information gathered would supplement that continuously being fed to the electoral roll. This would help to reduce errors, time delays, and possible confusion among voters on election day. Periodic door-to-door enumerations would enable Elections Canada to update and correct the existing Register. They would also offer voters the chance to bring their entry in the Register up to date and to learn more about the operation of the Register.

Glossary

alternative vote (AV). A preferential vote within single-member constituencies. Voters number all candidates preferentially. If no majority winner is chosen on the first count of the ballots, the candidate with the fewest first-choice preferences is eliminated. The second-choice preferences on those ballots are allocated amongst the remaining candidates. The process continues until a majority winner is declared (Australia, House of Representatives).

first past the post (FPTP). Technically a misnomer, for apart from having a minimum of one more votes than any other candidate, there is no "post" for the winner to pass. The candidate with the most votes, which is to say a plurality of the votes, is elected. An alternative term to FPTP to describe plurality voting is "single member plurality" (SMP) (Canada, House of Commons and all provincial legislatures).

Gini index. The Gini index is a statistical tool originally designed in economics to measure the inequality of income or consumption of a defined population. Applied to electoral districting, a Gini score of "0" indicates complete equality of population among the districts and a score of "1" complete inequality of population. (Explanations of the Gini Index are found in Alker 1965, ch 3.)

mixed-member proportional (MMP). A two-ballot electoral scheme. A proportion (usually one-half) of an assembly's members is elected in single-member districts by FPTP. The remaining members are elected from party lists in proportion to the share of votes received by a party for a region (or the whole country). This compensates for the disproportionality of a party's share of the seats in relation to its share of the votes in the plurality elections (Germany, Bundestag; New Zealand, House of Representatives).

plurality voting. See **first past the post.**

proportional representation (PR). A generic term for a method of election that attempts to convert a party's share of the votes into a close approximation of its share of assembly seats. Multimember constituencies, possibly as large as a single constituency for the entire country, are a requirement. The greater the number of members elected from a constituency the greater PR's capacity to translate votes into seats equitably.

single transferable vote (STV). Preferential voting in multimember districts. As with AV, voters rank the candidates according to their preference orderings.

Transfers of preference-ordered votes among the candidates in a district follow either from the gradual elimination of low-ranked candidates or from the distribution of votes that are "surplus" to the quota required to win a seat established for that district. The process continues until all members to which a district is entitled have been elected (Australia, Senate; Ireland, Dáil).

two-round (second round). Single-member district elections held, if no majority winner is declared on the first vote, a week or two after the first vote. Similar to runoff elections in American primaries, the second ballot may be open only to candidates who surpassed a threshold of votes established for the first ballot. The candidate with the largest share of the votes on the second ballot, whether a majority or not, is declared the winner (France, Chamber of Deputies).

Additional Reading

The twenty-three volumes of research studies conducted for the Royal Commission on Electoral Reform and Party Financing (RCERPF) constitute the most important set of works published in Canada on our parties, party system, voters, elections, and electoral institutions. The commission's four-volume *Report* and its collected *Research studies* all carry the publication date of 1991.

The history and content of Canada's electoral laws are documented in Patrick Boyer's *Election law in Canada: The law and procedure of federal and territorial elections* (1987). The links between Canada's electoral laws, parliamentary practices, and party system are addressed in my "Recognition of Canadian political parties in Parliament and in law" (1978). I also examined some legal aspects of our electoral institutions a decade following the adoption of the Canadian Charter of Rights and Freedoms in "Discrimination in Canada's electoral law" (1993).

The first serious study of voter registration in Canada was conducted by Canada's representation commissioner. His report to Parliament, entitled *Report of the representation commissioner on methods of registration of electors and absentee voting* (Representation Commissioner 1968), recommended against replacing door-to-door enumeration with a so-called permanent voters list. An earlier American study of alternative forms of registering voters also commented favourably on Canada's door-to-door enumeration system. It was carried out by the National Municipal League Elections Systems Project and was published as *Voter registration systems in Canada and Western Europe* (1974). Methods of registering voters at the federal level in Canada, in British Columbia, the United States, and the United Kingdom are evaluated in John C. Courtney, ed., *Registering voters: Comparative perspectives* (1991).

Several studies of electoral redistricting in Canada predated my *Commissioned ridings* (2001). Norman Ward was the first to examine in any systematic fashion the effect of the change from government-controlled redistributions to independent commissions in "A century of constituencies" (1967a). This was followed by R.K. Carty's "The electoral boundary revolution in Canada" (1985). The Supreme Court of Canada's ruling in the 1991 *Carter* reference is the subject of a book edited by John C. Courtney, Peter MacKinnon, and David E. Smith, *Drawing boundaries: Legislatures, courts, and electoral values* (1993).

I have contrasted electoral boundary readjustments in Canada and Australia in two studies. "'Theories masquerading as principles': Canadian electoral boundary commissions and the Australian model" (1985) examines the early years of independent redistributions in Australia and accounts for the choice that Manitoba, and later Canada, made in adopting the Australia's boundary readjustment mechanism. This study was followed by a comparative assessment of the two systems in "Electoral boundary redistributions: Contrasting approaches to parliamentary representation" (1992).

The debate over the links between Canada's electoral system, regionalized parties, and cabinet government was launched by Alan Cairns in "The electoral system and the party system in Canada, 1921-1965" (1968). It was joined by J.A.A. Lovink in "On analyzing the impact of the electoral system on the party system in Canada" (1970), with a reply from Cairns entitled "On analyzing the impact of the electoral system: A reply to J.A.A. Lovink" (1970). In "Cairns revisited: The electoral system and the party system in Canada" (1990) Nelson Wiseman adds a useful comment and update on the questions first raised by Cairns.

The best general, theoretical explorations of political representation are Hannah F. Pitkin's *The concept of representation* (1967) and A.H. Birch's *Representation* (1971). J. Paul Johnston and Harvey E. Pasis compiled a valuable collection of papers on representation in Canada in their edited book *Representation and electoral systems: Canadian perspectives* (1990).

Among the recent comparisons of methods of election are André Blais and R. Kenneth Carty, "The impact of electoral formulae on the creation of majority governments" (1987), André Blais and Louis Massicotte, "Electoral systems" (1996), and Pippa Norris, "Choosing electoral systems: Proportional, majoritarian and mixed systems" (1997).

There is a vast literature, parts of it dating back over a century, on the merits and faults of Canada's plurality vote system. The most important of the works to have appeared in the past decade, many of them favouring some alternative to first past the post, include the following: André Blais, "Rethinking our electoral system: The case for majority run-off elections" (1993), Law Commission of Canada, *Renewing democracy: debating electoral reform in Canada. A discussion paper* (2002), Henry Milner, ed., *Making votes count: Reassessing Canada's electoral system* (1999), F. Leslie Seidle, "The Canadian electoral system and proposals for reform" (1996) and *Electoral system reform in Canada: Objectives, advocacy and implications for government* (2002), Donley F. Studlar, "The last Westminster electoral system? Canada not Britain" (1998), R. Kent Weaver, *Electoral reform for the Canadian House of Commons* (1997) and "Electoral rules and electoral reform in Canada" (2001). Two issues of *Policy Options* have been devoted to an assessment of plurality voting in Canada: *Electoral reform/La réforme électorale* (1997) and *Votes and seats/Des votes et des sièges* (2001).

Part of the literature on electoral systems examines the strengths and weaknesses of various methods of election not discussed in this book. For useful book-length studies of all methods of election see Cox 1997; Farrell 1997; Farrell 2001; Grofman and Lijphart 1986; International IDEA 1997; Reilly 2001; and Shugart and Wattenberg 2001.

Works Cited

Alker, Hayward A. 1965. *Mathematics and politics.* New York: Macmillan.

Aucoin, Peter, and Jennifer Smith. 1997. Proportional representation: Misrepresenting equality. *Policy Options* 18(9): 30-2.

Balasko, Richard D. 1990. Brief to the Royal Commission on Electoral Reform and Party Financing. RCERPF files, Ottawa.

Birch, A.H. 1971. *Representation.* London: Macmillan.

Black, Jerome H. 2000. *The national register of electors: Raising questions about the new approach to voter registration in Canada.* Montreal: Institute for Research on Public Policy.

—. 2002. The permanent voters list vs. voter enumeration. Paper presented at the Transparency, Disclosure and Democracy Conference, Ottawa, ON, 27 February.

—. 2003. From enumeration to the national register of electors: An account and an evaluation. Occasional paper. *Choices* 9(7). Montreal: Institute for Research on Public Policy.

Blais, André. 1993. Rethinking our electoral system: The case for majority run-off elections. *Inroads* 2(1): 124-30.

Blais, André, and R. Kenneth Carty. 1987. The impact of electoral formulae on the creation of majority governments. *Electoral Studies* 6: 209-18.

—. 1990. Does proportional representation foster voter turnout? *European Journal of Political Research* 18(2): 167-82.

Blais, André, and Elisabeth Gidengil. 1991. *Making representative democracy work: The view of Canadians.* Vol. 17 of *Research studies for the Royal Commission on Electoral Reform and Party Financing.* Toronto: Dundurn Press.

Blais, André, Elisabeth Gidengil, Richard Nadeau, and Neil Nevitte. 2002. *Anatomy of a liberal victory: Making sense of the vote in the 2000 Canadian election.* Peterborough, ON: Broadview Press.

Blais, André, Elisabeth Gidengil, Neil Nevitte, and Richard Nadeau. 2001. The evolving nature of non-voting: Evidence from Canada. Paper presented at the annual meeting of the American Political Science Association, San Francisco, CA, 30 August-2 September.

Blais, André, and Louis Massicotte. 1996. Electoral systems. In *Comparing democracies,* ed. Lawrence LeDuc, Richard Niemi, and Pippa Norris, 49-82. Thousand Oaks, CA: Sage.

Bogdanor, Vernon. 1984. *What is proportional representation? A guide to the issues*. Oxford: Robertson.

Boix, Charles. 1999. Setting the rules of the game: The choice of electoral systems in advanced democracies. *American Political Science Review* 93(3): 609-24.

Boyer, J. Patrick. 1987. *Election law in Canada: The law and procedure of federal and territorial elections*. Toronto: Butterworth.

British North America Act, 1867. 30 and 31 Victoria. c. 3.

Burke, Edmund. 1996. Speech at the conclusion of the poll, 1774. In *The writings and speeches of Edmund Burke: Party, Parliament and the American war, 1774-1780*, ed. Warrant M. Elofson with John A. Woods III, 64-70. Oxford: Clarendon Press.

Bystydzienski, Jill M. 1994. Norway: Achieving world-record women's representation in government. In *Electoral systems in comparative perspective: Their impact on women and minorities*, ed. Wilma Rule and Joseph F. Zimmerman, 55-64. London: Greenwood Press.

—. 1995. *Women in electoral politics: Lessons from Norway*. Westport, CT: Praeger.

Cairns, Alan. 1968. The electoral system and the party system in Canada, 1921-1965. *Canadian Journal of Political Science* 1(1): 55-80.

—. 1970. On analyzing the impact of the electoral system: A reply to J.A.A. Lovink. *Canadian Journal of Political Science* 3(4): 517-21.

Cameron, Barbara. 2002. It's not enough, Mr. Martin. *Globe and Mail*, 24 October, A20.

Canadian Disability Rights Council v. Canada. 1988. 3 F.C. 622 (T.D.).

Carty, R.K. 1985. The electoral boundary revolution in Canada. *American Review of Canadian Studies* 15(3): 273-87.

—. 1988. Campaigning in the trenches: The transformation of constituency politics. In *Party democracy in Canada: The politics of national party conventions*, ed. G.C. Perlin, 84-96. Scarborough, ON: Prentice-Hall.

Carty, R.K., William Cross, and Lisa Young. 2000. *Rebuilding Canadian party politics*. Vancouver: UBC Press.

Chief Electoral Officer. *Reports*. Ottawa. 1953-2000.

Cleverdon, Catherine L. 1974. *The woman suffrage movement in Canada*. Toronto: University of Toronto Press.

Courtney, John C. 1978. Recognition of Canadian political parties in Parliament and in law. *Canadian Journal of Political Science* 15(1): 33-60.

—. 1980. Reflections on reforming the Canadian electoral system. *Canadian Public Administration* 23(3): 427-57.

—. 1985. "Theories masquerading as principles": Canadian electoral boundary commissions and the Australian model. In *The Canadian House of Commons: Essays in honour of Norman Ward,* ed. John C. Courtney, 135-71. Calgary: University of Calgary Press.

—. 1992. Electoral boundary redistributions: Contrasting approaches to parliamentary representation. In *Comparative political studies: Australia and Canada,* ed. Malcolm Alexander and Brian Galligan, 45-58. Melbourne: Longmans Cheshire.

—. 1993. Discrimination in Canada's electoral law. In *Discrimination in the law in the administration of justice,* ed. Walter Tarnopolsky, Joyce Whitman, and Monique Ouellette, 401-10. Toronto: Carswell.

—. 1995. *Do conventions matter? Choosing national party leaders in Canada.* Montreal: McGill-Queen's University Press.

—. 1999. Electoral reform and Canada's parties. In *Making every vote count: Reassessing Canada's electoral system,* ed. Henry Milner, 91-100. Peterborough, ON: Broadview Press.

—. 2001. *Commissioned ridings: Designing Canada's electoral districts.* Montreal: McGill-Queen's University Press.

—, ed. 1991. *Registering voters: Comparative perspectives.* Cambridge, MA: Harvard University Center for International Affairs.

Courtney, John C., Peter MacKinnon, and David E. Smith, eds. 1993. *Drawing boundaries: Legislatures, courts, and electoral values.* Saskatoon: Fifth House.

Courtney, John C., and David E. Smith. 1991. Registering voters: Canada in a comparative context. In *Democratic rights and electoral reform,* ed. Michael Cassidy, 343-461. Vol. 10 of *Research studies for the Royal Commission on Electoral Reform and Party Financing.* Toronto: Dundurn Press.

Cox, Gary W. 1997. *Making votes count: Strategic coordination in the world's electoral systems.* New York: Cambridge University Press.

Coyne, Andrew. 2000. The right to vote, and the obligation. *National Post,* 20 December, A20.

Cross, William. 2004. *Political parties.* Vancouver: UBC Press.

Cuneo, Carl. 2002. Globalized and localized digital divides along the information highway: A fragile synthesis across bridges, ramps, cloverleaves, and ladders. 33rd Annual Sorokin Lecture, University of Saskatchewan, 31 January.

Cyber balloting proposed to entice youth to vote. 2002. Saskatoon *StarPhoenix,* 22 January, C10.

Davis, Morris. 1967. Ballot behaviour in Halifax revisited. In *Voting in Canada,* ed. John C. Courtney, 130-42. Toronto: Prentice-Hall.

Dawson, Robert MacGregor. 1947. *The government of Canada*. Toronto: University of Toronto Press.

Dembart, Lee. 2003. Are Internet ballots a vote-fixer's dream? *International Herald Tribune*, 28 April, 1 and 6.

Denemark, David, 1998. Campaign activities and marginality. In *Voters' victory: New Zealand's first election under proportional representation,* ed. Jack Vowles, Peter Aimer, Susan Banducci, and Jeffrey Karp, 81-100. Auckland, NZ: University of Auckland Press.

Dickinson, P., and J. Ellison. 2000. Plugging in: The increase of household Internet use continues into 1999. Occasional paper. Statistics Canada. 1 November.

Docherty, David. 1997. *Mr. Smith goes to Ottawa: Life in the House of Commons.* Vancouver: UBC Press.

Donnelly, M.S. 1957. Parliamentary government in Manitoba. *Canadian Journal of Economics and Political Science* 23(1): 20-32.

—. 1963. *The government of Manitoba*. Toronto: University of Toronto Press.

Edwards v. A.G. for Canada. [1930]. A.C. 124.

Elections BC. 1999. *Report of the chief electoral officer on the 1999 provincial enumeration*. Victoria: Elections BC.

Elections Canada. 1997. *Official voting results: 36th general election*. Ottawa: Elections Canada.

—. 2000a. *Report of the chief electoral officer of Canada on the 36th general election.*

—. 2000b. *2000 general election post-event overview.* Ottawa: Elections Canada.

—. 2001a. *Modernizing the electoral process: Recommendations from the chief electoral officer of Canada following the 37th general election*. Ottawa: Elections Canada.

—. 2001b. *Performance report*. Ottawa: Elections Canada.

—. 2001c. *Report of the chief electoral officer of Canada on the 37th general election held on November 27, 2000*. Ottawa: Elections Canada.

—. 2002. Information provided by Rennie Molnar, Director, Register, Geography and Information Technology, Elections Canada, 11 October.

Electoral reform/La réforme électorale. 1997. *Policy Options* 18(9).

Farrell, David M. 1997. *Comparing electoral systems*. New York: Prentice Hall/Harvester Wheatsheaf.

—. 2001. *Electoral systems: A comparative introduction*. New York: Palgrave.

Forsey, Eugene. 1963. Government defeats in the Canadian House of Commons, 1867-73. *Canadian Journal of Economics and Political Science* 23(3): 364-7.

Frizzell, Alan, and Anthony Westell. 1994. The press and the prime minister. In *The Canadian general election of 1993,* ed. Alan Frizzell, Jon H. Pammett, and Anthony Westell, 89-106. Ottawa: Carleton University Press.

Garner, John. 1969. *The franchise and politics in British North America, 1755-1867.* Toronto: University of Toronto Press.

Gidengil, Elisabeth, André Blais, Neil Nevitte, and Richard Nadeau, 2004. *Citizens.* Vancouver: UBC Press.

Grofman, Bernard, and Arend Lijphart, eds. 1986. *Electoral laws and their political consequences.* New York: Agathon Press.

Grose, Christian R., and Antoine Yoshinaka, 2002. Electoral institutions and voter participation: The effect of felon disfranchisement laws on voter turnout in the US southern states, 1984-2000. Paper presented at the annual general meeting of the Canadian Political Science Association, Toronto, ON, 29-31 May.

House of Commons. 1920. *Debates.* Hugh Guthrie, Minister of Militia and Acting Solicitor General, 11 March.

—. 1939. *Debates.* C.G. Power, 13 March.

Ibbitson, John. 2002. Restoring the dignity of Parliament. *Globe and Mail,* 22 October, A4.

International IDEA. 1997. *Handbook of electoral system design.* Stockholm: International Institute for Democracy and Electoral Assistance.

Inter-Parliamentary Union. 2001. Women in national parliaments. <www.ipu.org/wmn-e/classif.htm>. 14 August 2001.

Johnston, J. Paul, and Harvey E. Pasis, eds. 1990. *Representation and electoral systems: Canadian perspectives.* Toronto: Prentice-Hall.

Johnston, Richard. 2001. A conservative case for electoral reform. *Policy Options* 22(6): 7-15.

Judge, David. 1999. *Representation: Theory and practice in Britain.* London: Routledge.

Kingsley, Jean-Pierre. 2001. Independence and accountability mechanisms in federal election legislation. Paper presented at the Conference on Independence and Responsibility: Canada's Officers of Parliament, Saskatoon, SK, 2-3 November.

KPMG/Sussex Circle. 1998. *Technology and the voting process: Final report prepared for Elections Canada.* 15 June.

Law Commission of Canada. 2002. *Renewing democracy: Debating electoral reform in Canada. A discussion paper.* Ottawa: Law Commission of Canada.

Legislative Assembly of the Province of Canada. 1866. *Scrapbook Hansard/Parliamentary Debates Recorded in Newspaper,* 13 July.

Lovink, J.A.A. 1970. On analyzing the impact of the electoral system on the party system in Canada. *Canadian Journal of Political Science* 3(4): 497-516.

LeDuc, Lawrence, and Jon H. Pammett. 2003. Elections and participation: The meanings of the turnout decline. Paper presented at the annual general meeting of the Canadian Political Science Association, Halifax, NS, 1 June.

Mair, Peter. 1986. Districting choices under the single-transferable vote. In *Electoral laws and their political consequences,* ed. Bernard Grofman and Arend Lijphart, 289-307. New York: Agathon Press.

Massicotte, Louis. 2001. Refereeing the political process: The chief electoral officer of Canada. Paper presented at the Conference on Independence and Responsibility: Canada's Officers of Parliament, Saskatoon, SK, 2-3 November.

Milner, Henry, ed. 1999. *Making votes count: Reassessing Canada's electoral system*. Peterborough, ON: Broadview Press.

Minister of Public Works. 1997. *A history of the vote in Canada,* Ottawa: Minister of Public Works and Government Services Canada.

Morton, W.L. 1957. *Manitoba: A history.* Toronto: University of Toronto Press.

Muldoon v. Canada 1988. [3 F.C.] 628-36.

National Municipal League Elections Systems Project. 1974. *Voter registration systems in Canada and Western Europe*. New York: National Municipal League.

N.B. Native chiefs criticize idea to pool federal Native vote. 2002. Halifax *Chronicle-Herald,* 3 July, D11.

Norris, Pippa. 1997. Choosing electoral systems: Proportional, majoritarian and mixed systems. *International Political Science Review* 18(3): 297-312.

Nova Scotia Electoral Boundaries Commission. 1992. *Effective political representation in Nova Scotia: The 1992 report of the provincial electoral boundaries commission.* Halifax: Queen's Printer.

Pitkin, Hanna Fenichel. 1967. *The concept of representation.* Berkeley: University of California Press.

Prentice, Alison, Paula Bourne, Gail Cuthbert Brandt, Beth Light, Wendy Mitchinson, Naomi Black. 1988. *Canadian women: A history.* Toronto: Harcourt Brace Jovanovich.

Putnam, Robert. 2000. *Bowling alone: The collapse and revival of American community.* New York: Simon and Schuster.

Qualter, T.H. 1970. *The electoral process in Canada.* Toronto: McGraw-Hill.

RCERPF (Royal Commission on Electoral Reform and Party Financing). 1991a. *Reforming electoral democracy.* Vol. 1. Ottawa: Supply and Services.

—. 1991b. *Report.* 4 vols. Toronto: Dundurn Press.

—. 1991c. *Research studies.* 23 vols. Toronto: Dundurn Press.

Rebick, Judy. 2001. PR can help solve Canada's democracy deficit. *Policy Options* 22(6): 15-16.

Reference re: Provincial Election Boundaries. 1991. (SASK) 5 W.W.R.

Reid v. Canada (1994), 73 F.T.R. 290 (T.D.).

Reilly, Benjamin. 2001. *Democracy in divided societies: Electoral engineering for conflict management.* Cambridge: Cambridge University Press.

Report of the Chief Electoral Officer of Canada. 1997. Ottawa: Elections Canada.

Representation Commissioner. 1968. *Report of the representation commissioner on methods of registration of electors and absentee voting.* Ottawa: Queen's Printer.

Roy, Patricia E. 1981. Citizens without votes: East Asians in British Columbia, 1872-1947. In *Ethnicity, power and politics in Canada,* ed. Jorgen Dalhie and Tessa Fernando, 151-71. Toronto: Methuen.

Royal Commission on the Electoral System. 1986. *Towards a better democracy: Report of the Royal Commission on the Electoral System.* Wellington, NZ: Government Printer.

Rule, Wilma. 1994. Parliaments of, by and for the people: Except for women? In *Electoral systems in comparative perspective: Their impact on women and minorities,* ed. Wilma Rule and Joseph F. Zimmerman, 15-30. London: Greenwood Press.

Russow, Joan, and Green Party of Canada v. A.G. Canada. 2001. Application record, including factum, filed with the Ontario Superior Court of Justice, 1 May.

Sauvé v. Canada (A.G.) (1992), 89 D.L.R. (4th) 644 (Ont. C.A.); appeal dismissed (1993) 2 S.C.R. 438, 153 N.R. 242 (S.C.C.).

Sauvé v. Canada [Chief Electoral Officer]. (2002) S.C.C. 68.

Schindeler, F.F. 1969. *Responsible government in Ontario.* Toronto: University of Toronto Press.

Schouls, Tim. 1996. Aboriginal peoples and electoral reform in Canada: Differentiated representation versus voter equality. *Canadian Journal of Political Science* 29(4): 729-49.

Schumpeter, Joseph A. 1962. *Capitalism, socialism and democracy.* 3d ed. New York: Harper and Row.

Seidle, F. Leslie. 1996. The Canadian electoral system and proposals for reform. In *Canadian Parties in Transition,* ed. A. Brian Tanguay and Alain-G. Gagnon, 282-306. 2d ed. Toronto: Nelson Canada.

—. 2002. *Electoral system reform in Canada: Objectives, advocacy and implications for government.* Ottawa: Canadian Policy Research Networks Inc., prepared for the Law Commission of Canada.

Shugart, Matthew Soberg, and Martin P. Wattenberg, eds. *Mixed-member electoral systems: The best of both worlds?* New York: Oxford University Press.

Simpson, Jeffrey. 2002. We need all hands on deck. *Globe and Mail,* 1 February, A13.

Smith, David. 1991. Federal voter enumeration in Canada: An assessment. In *Registering voters: A comparative perspective,* ed. John C. Courtney, 35-40. Cambridge, MA: Center for International Affairs, Harvard University.

Speech from the Throne, 1969. 28th Parliament. 2nd session. House of Commons. *Debates*, p. 2.

Statistics Canada. 2001. *Changing our ways: Why and how Canadians use the Internet*, 26 March.

Statutes of Quebec. 1979. An act respecting electoral representation, c. 57.

Studlar, Donley T. 1998. The last Westminster electoral system? Canada not Britain. *Representation* 35(1): 70-8.

Swinton, Katherine. 1992. Federalism, representation, and rights. In *Drawing boundaries: legislatures, courts, and electoral values,* ed. John C. Courtney, Peter MacKinnon, and David E. Smith, 17-39. Saskatoon: Fifth House Publishers.

Teixeira, Ruy A. 1987. *Why Americans don't vote: Turnout decline in the United States, 1960-1984.* Westport, CT: Greenwood Press.

Votes and seats/Des votes et des sièges. 2001. *Policy Options* 22(6).

Vowles, Jack. 2002. Offsetting the PR effect? Party mobilization and turnout decline in New Zealand, 1996-99. *Party Politics* 8(5): 587-605.

Ward, Norman. 1950. *Canadian House of Commons: Representation.* Toronto: University of Toronto Press.

—. 1967a. A century of constituencies. *Canadian Public Administration* 10(1): 105-21.

—. 1967b. Voting in Canadian two-member constituencies. In *Voting in Canada,* ed. John C. Courtney, 125-9. Toronto: Prentice-Hall of Canada.

Weaver, R. Kent. 1997. Electoral reform for the Canadian house of commons. *Canadian Journal of Political Science* 33(3): 473-512.

—. 2001. Electoral rules and electoral reform in Canada. In *Mixed-member electoral systems: The best of both worlds?* ed. Matthew Soberg Shugart and Martin P. Wattenberg, 542-96. New York: Oxford University Press.

White, Graham. 2002. Sandbagging the permanent voters' list. Paper presented at the Transparency, Disclosure and Democracy Conference, Ottawa, ON, 27 February.

Wiseman, Nelson. 1991. Cairns revisited: The electoral system and the party system in Canada. In *Politics: Canada,* ed. Paul Fox and Graham White, 265-74. 7th ed. Toronto: McGraw-Hill Ryerson.

Wolfinger, Raymond E., Benjamin Highton, and Megan Mullin. 2002. *Between registering and voting: How state laws affect the turnout of young registrants.* Paper presented at the annual meeting of the American Political Science Association, Boston, MA, 29 August-1 September.

Young, Lisa. 1997. Gender equal legislatures: Evaluating the proposed Nunavut electoral system. *Canadian Public Policy* 23(3): 306-15.

Zimmerman, Joseph F. 1994. Equity in representation for women and minorities. In *Electoral systems in comparative perspective: Their impact on women and minorities,* ed. Wilma Rule and Joseph F. Zimmerman, 3-13. London: Greenwood Press.

Index

A master index to all volumes in the Canadian Democratic Audit series can be found at www.ubcpress.ca/readingroom/audit/index.

Copy editor: Sarah Wight

Text design: Peter Ross, Counterpunch

Typesetter: Artegraphica Design Co. Ltd.

Proofreader: Tara Tovell

Indexer: Geri Rowlatt